Imago Christi

THE EXAMPLE OF JESUS CHRIST

JAMES STALKER

BJU PRESS

GREENVILLE, SOUTH CAROLINA

Library of Congress Cataloging-in-Publication Data

Stalker, James, 1848-1927.
   Imago Christi : the example of Jesus Christ / James Stalker.
     p. cm.
   Originally published: New York : A. C. Armstrong & Son, 1889.
   ISBN 1-57924-853-5 (alk. paper)
   1. Jesus Christ—Example. 2. Jesus Christ—Ethics. I. Title.
   BT304 .S8 2002
   232.9'04—dc21

                    2002007233

Cover and title page: *The Ascension* by Gustave Doré. From the
Bob Jones University Collection.

All Scripture is quoted from the Authorized King James Version.

Imago Christi: The Example of Jesus Christ
James Stalker

Design by Jeff Gray
Composition by Kelley Moore

© 2002 by Bob Jones University Press
Greenville, South Carolina 29614

Printed in the United States of America

ISBN 1-57924-853-5

14   13   12   11   10   9   8   7   6   5   4   3   2   1

Contents

Introduction

The author of the following volume is one of the most eminent of the younger ministers of the Free Church of Scotland. Educated in his native land, he spent some time in Germany, prosecuting there such studies as he judged to be best fitted to prepare him for his life-work in the ministry of the gospel.

He began his pastoral labors in Kirkcaldy, Fifeshire, and while there attracted wide attention by his eloquence as a preacher and his excellence as an expositor of the Word of God. Two or three years ago he was called to Free St. Matthew's Church, Glasgow, where by all he is "esteemed very highly in love for his work's sake." He occupies there a place of commanding influence, and by his labors among young people and his active sympathy with evangelistic work, he is proving himself eminently useful.

All who were present at the Belfast meeting of the Presbyterian Alliance recognized his ability in dealing with a difficult subject; and his volumes on the "Life of Christ" and the "Life of St. Paul," though issued under the unpretending title of handbooks, are remarkable for their originality of method, clearness of style, comprehensiveness of view, and suggestiveness of matter.

The same qualities are conspicuous in his treatment, in "Imago Christi," of the example of Christ, a subject which he has handled in a way entirely his own and in a spirit of devoutest reverence. We commend the work as equally fitted to be a companion for the closet and a directory for the life.

WM. M. TAYLOR.

New York, Nov. 23, 1889.

If it were permissible, I could truly describe the origin of this book in the very words of Bunyan:

> When at the first I took my pen in hand
> Thus for to write, I did not understand
> That I at all should make a little book
> In such a mode; nay, I had undertook
> To make another; which, when almost done,
> Before I was aware, I this begun.

Whilst writing my *Life of Christ,* and reading extensively on the subject, the conviction was borne in upon me that no desideratum more urgently needs to be supplied in our theology than a work on the Mind or Teaching of Christ. For several years I have been working at this task. But, as I went on, my progress was impeded by the fact that, especially in the department of ethics, Jesus seemed to teach as much by His example as by His words; whereas it was my intention to derive His teaching from His words alone. I commenced accordingly to write a little on His example, merely for the purpose of clearing the surplus material out of the way, and without any thought that it would expand beyond a chapter or two. But, as I wrote, it grew and grew, till, almost unawares, the plan of a new book shaped itself in my mind. Recurring to the quaint and pithy language of Bunyan, I may say:

> Having now my method by the end,
> Still, as I pulled, it came; and so I penned
> It down; until it came at last to be,
> For length and breadth, the bigness which you see.

The plan of this book, as it thus, so to speak, made itself, is—to divide the circle of human life into segments, each of which represents an extensive sphere of experience and duty, and then to follow our Lord through them one after another, in order to see how He conducted Himself in each and thereby learn how to conduct ourselves in the same. It is thus a kind of Christian Ethics with a practical and devotional aim. By making the segments smaller, the chapters might easily have increased in number; but perhaps no very important part of life has been entirely overlooked. Each chapter has been written in full view of the whole of our Lord's behavior, as far as it has been recorded, in the department of human life to which it refers; and it was at one time my intention to print in full, from the Gospels, all the evidence on each head. I soon found, however, that this would be impracticable, for the evidence turned out to be far more voluminous than I had any conception of; and to print it in full would have swelled the book to double its size. It has been to me a continual astonishment to find how abundant are the materials for tracing out our Lord's example even in what may be considered the less important aspects of life; and I thankfully confess that I have derived from this study a new impression of the wealth which is packed into the narrow circumference of the Four Gospels. On the flyleaf of each chapter I have noted a number of the more important passages; and this list, although in no case complete, may serve as a starting-point to those who may wish to collect the evidence for themselves.

I am persuaded that there are many at present in all the churches who are turning earnest eyes to the example of Christ, and who desire an account, derived directly from the records, of how He lived this earthly life which we are living now. They have awakened to the value and solemnity of the time, and feel that the one thing needful is to fill our few and swiftly passing years with a life large and useful and ever more abundant. But it must be a life like Christ's, for His was the best; and any life, however filled with excitement or success, of which He disapproved, would not seem to them worth living. For such I have written this guide to the imitation of Christ, and I send it forth with the earnest hope that they may be able to find in it, in some degree, the authentic features of the image of the Son of man.

GLASGOW, September 2nd, 1889.

I.

Introductory:

THOMAS À KEMPIS' *IMITATION OF CHRIST*

But *Thomas À Kempis?*—*the name had come across her in her reading, and she felt the satisfaction, which every one knows, of getting some ideas to attach to a name that strays solitary in the memory. She took up the little old clumsy book with some curiosity: it had the corners turned down in many places, and some hand, now for ever quiet, had made at certain passages strong pen-and-ink marks, long since browned by time. Maggie turned from leaf to leaf, and read where the quiet hand pointed. . . .*

A strange thrill of awe passed through her while she read, as if she had been wakened in the night by a strain of solemn music, telling of beings whose souls had been astir while hers was in stupor. . . . She knew nothing of doctrines and systems—of mysticism or quietism; but this voice out of the far-off middle ages was the direct communication of a human soul's belief and experience, and came to her as an unquestioned message.

I suppose that is the reason why the small old-fashioned book, for which you need only pay sixpence at a bookstall, works miracles to this day, turning bitter waters into sweetness; while expensive sermons and treatises, newly issued, leave all things as they were before. It was written down by a hand that waited for the heart's prompting; it is the chronicle of a solitary, hidden anguish, struggle, trust, and triumph—not written on velvet cushions to teach endurance to those who are treading with bleeding feet on the stones. And so it remains to all time a lasting record of human needs and human consolations.

GEORGE ELIOT: *The Mill on the Floss*

CHAPTER I.

Introductory.

THOMAS À KEMPIS' *IMITATION OF CHRIST.*

No religious book perhaps, outside the canon of Scripture, has attained so wide a diffusion in the Christian Church as the *De Imitatione Christi* of Thomas à Kempis. The only other book which may possibly compete with it in popularity is the *Pilgrim's Progress*. But the hold on Christendom of the older work is probably more extensive than even that of Bunyan's masterpiece; for, whilst the picture of Giant Pope must be an obstacle to the access of the *Pilgrim* to sensitive Catholics, the *Imitation* is as much read among Protestants as in the Church which claims it as its own, and in the Greek Church it is as popular as in either of the communions of the West.

I.

To Protestants it has a peculiar interest from the very fact that it was not written by the pen of a Protestant. It belongs to the beginning of the fifteenth century, and its author flourished a hundred years before Luther. It thus belongs to the age which must be accounted the darkest in the whole history of Christianity, when the light of God was well-nigh extinguished by the errors of men. Protestants, indeed, hardly think of the century before the Reformation as a time when Christianity existed at all; so vast is the accumulation of corruptions which meets the eye, that the religion of Christ almost seems to have disappeared. But this single book corrects this impression. The *Imitation of Christ* is a voice rising out of the darkness to remind us that the Church of Christ never ceased to exist, but that God had His witnesses and Christ His lovers even in the era of deepest decay.

The *Imitation* itself, indeed, bears marks of the evil time in which it arose. There are elements of superstition in it which the modern mind rejects. But these relics of a corrupt age only make the profoundly Christian tone of the whole the more surprising. It throbs throughout with a devotion to Christ which will find its way to the hearts of Christians in every age:

> O my beloved Spouse Christ Jesus, most pure Lover, Ruler of all creation, who will give me the wings of true liberty to fly and repose in Thee?
>
> O Jesus, Brightness of the eternal glory, Comfort of the pilgrim soul, with Thee are my lips without a voice, and my very silence speaks to Thee.
>
> How long delays my Lord His coming? Let Him come to me, His poor servant, and make me glad. Come, come, for without Thee there will be no glad day nor hour; for Thou art my gladness, and without Thee my table is unspread.
>
> Let others seek, instead of Thee, whatever else they please; nothing else pleases me, or shall please me, but Thou, my God, my Hope, my Eternal Salvation.

The book overflows with love to the Saviour expressed in this impassioned strain; and one very remarkable thing is that, on the whole, the soul goes straight to Christ without halting at those means of grace which were at that time so often substituted for the Saviour or feeling any need of the intercession of the Virgin or the saints, on which so much stress is laid in Catholic books of devotion. This is the healthiest feature of the whole production and must be welcome to every one who wishes to believe that even in that age, when the spirit was buried beneath the forms of worship, there were many souls that reached up through all obstacles to contact with the living Saviour.

II.

Obscure as is the external history of the author of the *Imitation*,* the reader comes to be on the most intimate terms with him. He is a mere shadow to the scientific historian; but to the devout student his personality is most distinct; his accent is separate and easily detected; and, notwithstanding the flight and passion of his devotion, there is in him something homely and kindly that wins our affection. Above all, we feel, as we open the book, that we are entering into communion with one who has found the secret of life. Here is one who, after weary wanderings, such as we perhaps are still entangled in, and many conflicts, such as we may still be waging, has attained the peace of God; and he takes us aside and leads us by the hand to view the land

---

* "The writer of the *Imitatio Christi* is not known, and perhaps never will be known, with absolute certainty. The dispute about the authorship has filled a hundred volumes, and is still so undecided that the voice of the sweetest and humblest of books has come to us mingled, for the last two and a half centuries, with one of the most bitter and arrogant of literary controversies. . . . Of the nine or ten saints and doctors to whom at different times the work has been attributed, the pretensions of three alone can be now said to possess the least germ of probability. These three are a certain Gersen de Cabanis, Thomas Hemerken of Kempen, and Jean de Charlier de Gerson; and the claims of the first of the three . . . may now be considered to be set at rest.

"The two, then, between whom rests the glory of the authorship—though in truth earthly glory was the last thing for which the author would have wished— are *Thomas à Kempis*, sub-prior of the monastery of St. Agnes, in the diocese of Cologne, and *Jean Gerson*, Chancellor of the University of Paris, and one of the grandest figures of his time.

"The lives of both these saints of God fell in the same dreary epoch. It was that 'age of lead and iron,' of political anarchy and ecclesiastical degradation, of war, famine, misery, agitation, corruption, which marked the close of the fourteenth and the beginning of the fifteenth century. Thomas à Kempis, born in 1379, died at the age of ninety-two; Gerson, born in 1363, died at the age of sixty-one. They were thus contemporaries for forty-five years of their lives. But the destinies of the two men were utterly different.

"Thomas, the son of an artisan, a quiet recluse, a copier of manuscripts, was trained at Deventer, and was received into a monastery in the year 1400 at the

of rest. This is the enduring charm of the book. We all carry in our hearts a secret belief that somewhere in the world there exists a paradise unvexed with the cares by which we are pursued and watered by the river of God; and whenever one appears whose air assures us that he has lived in that Eden and drunk of that river, we cannot help welcoming him and listening to his message.

But where is this happy land? It is not far away. It is in ourselves: "The kingdom of God is within you." Men seek happiness out of themselves—in riches or learning or fame, in friendships and family connections, in talking about others and hearing news. They roam the world in search of adventures; they descend to the bottom of the sea and tear out the bowels of the earth in pursuit of wealth; they are driven forth by turbulent passions in search of excitement and novelty; they fight with one another, because every one, dissatisfied himself, believes that his brother is making away with his share. But all the time they are stumbling over their happiness, which lies among their feet; they fly to the ends of the earth in search of it, and lo it is at home.

> Whensoever a man desires anything inordinately, he is presently disquieted within himself. The proud and covetous are never at rest. The poor and humble in spirit live in abundance of peace.

---

age of twenty-one. In that monastery of St. Agnes—*valde devotus, libenter solus, nunquam otiosus*—he spent seventy-one years of perfect calm, unbroken except by one brief period, in which he fled from his cell rather than acknowledge an archbishop to whom the Pope had refused the pallium. This was almost the sole event of a life in which we are told that it was his chief delight to be alone in *angello cum libello*.

"Far different from this life, 'in a little corner with a little book,' was the troubled, prominent, impassioned life of *Jean Gerson*, the *Doctor Christianissimus*. Rising while yet young to a leading position, he was appointed Chancellor of the University of Paris before the age of thirty, and, struggling against popes and councils, and mobs and kings, became the stormiest champion of a stormy time. . . . And when all his life seemed to have culminated in one long failure . . . then forced to see how utterly little is man even at his greatest, and how different are the ways of man's nothing-perfectness from those of God's all-completeness, the great Chancellor, who has been the soul of mighty councils and the terror of

We might have much peace, if we would not busy ourselves with the sayings and doings of others, and with things which are no concern of ours.

How can he remain long in peace who entangles himself with the cares of others; who seeks occasions of going abroad, and is little or seldom inwardly recollected?

First keep thyself in peace, and then thou wilt be able to bring others to peace.

A good peaceable man turns all things to good. Such an one is conqueror of himself, and lord of the world, a friend of Christ, and an heir of heaven.

These counsels sound like many that the world has heard from others of its teachers. They sound like the doctrines of the Stoic philosophers, which ended in making self an arrogant little god; they sound like the teaching of some in modern times who, looking on the raising of "the pyramid of their own being" as the chief end of existence, have sacrificed to culture the rights of others and the most sacred obligations of morality. The doctrine that the interior man is the supreme object of care may turn into a doctrine of arrogant selfishness. But à Kempis has guarded well against this perversion. He has no maxims more pungent than those directed against the undue exaltation of self. When he

---

contumacious popes, takes obscure refuge, first in a monastery of Tyrol, afterwards under the rule of his brother at Lyons, and there, among the strict and humble Celestine monks, passes his last days in humility and submission. Far other thoughts than those of his tumultuous life had been revealed to him as he wandered, in danger and privation, among the mountains of Bavaria,—or, rather, those earlier objects had faded from the horizon of his soul like the burning hues of a stormy sunset; but as, when the sunset crimson has faded, we see the light of the eternal stars, so when the painted vapours of earthly ambition had lost their colouring, Gerson could gaze at last on those 'living sapphires' which glow in the deep firmament of spiritual hopes. He had been a leader among the schoolmen, now he cares only for the simplest truths. He had been a fierce gladiator in the arena of publicity, now he has passed into the life of holy silence. At his hottest period of strife he had cried out, 'Peace, peace, I long for peace;' now at last there has fallen on his soul—not as the world giveth—that peace that passeth understanding." FARRAR in *Companions of the Devout Life.*

advises us to turn away from outward things to seek the true wealth and happiness within, it is not in ourselves we are to find it, though it is within ourselves. We have to make an empty space within, that it may be filled with God, who is the only true satisfaction of the soul:

Know that the love of thyself doth hurt thee more than anything else in the world.

On this defect, that a man inordinately loves himself, hangs almost all in thee that thou hast to root out and overcome; and, when this evil has been once conquered and brought under, soon will there be great peace and tranquillity.

Christ will come to thee, holding out to thee His consolation, if thou prepare Him a fit dwelling within thee.

Many a visit does He make to the interior man; sweet is His communication with him, delightful His consolation, great His peace, and His familiarity exceedingly amazing. Give place, then, for Christ, and deny entrance to all others.

When thou hast Christ thou art rich, and He is sufficient for thee. He will provide for thee and faithfully supply thy wants in all things, so that thou needest not trust to men.

"Son," says Christ to us, "leave thyself, and thou shalt find Me."

III.

The merits of à Kempis are inimitable and imperishable; yet the book is not without defects more or less inseparable from the time and the circumstances in which it was written.

1. There is a defect of the *Imitation* which lies on the surface and has been often pointed out. Its author was a monk and needed a rule only for the little, monotonous world of the cloister; we

live in the freedom and amidst the perils of a larger world, which needs an example more universal. To à Kempis and his brethren this world was the territory of the Evil One, from which they had fled; they wished to have no dealings with it and had no hope of making it better. "Thou oughtest," he says, "to be so far dead to the affections of men as to wish, as far as thou canst, to be without any human company." Even life itself appeared to him an evil: in one of his gloomiest pages he says expressly, "It is truly a misery to live upon earth." This happily is not our creed,

> The world is not a blank to us,
> Nor blot; it means intensely, and means good.

To us it is God's world; and our vocation is to make God's will be done in all departments of its life and to make His Word run on all its highways and bye-ways. Monasticism was a confession on the part of Christianity of being beaten by the world; but to-day Christianity is planting its standard on every shore and going forth conquering and to conquer.

2. Another blemish which has been attributed to it is thus dealt with by Dr. Chalmers in one of his published Letters: "I have been reading Thomas à Kempis recently on the Imitation of Jesus Christ—a very impressive performance. Some would say of it that it is not enough evangelical. He certainly does not often affirm, in a direct and ostensible manner, the righteousness that is by faith. But he proceeds on this doctrine, and many an incidental recognition does he bestow upon it; and I am not sure but that this implies a stronger and more habitual settlement of mind respecting it than when it is thrust forward and repeated, and re-repeated with a kind of ultra-orthodoxy, as if to vindicate one's soundness, and acquit oneself of a kind of exacted homage to the form of sound words."*

This is both a generous and a just statement of à Kempis' position; though a simpler explanation of it lies in the fact that he

---

* *Correspondence of Rev. Thomas Chalmers, D.D.,* p. 81.

lived a hundred years before the republication, at the Reformation, of this cardinal doctrine of the Pauline theology. But it is a point of the greatest practical importance to emphasize that in experience the true order is, that the imitation of Christ should follow the forgiveness of sins through the blood of His cross.*

3. There is another great Pauline doctrine which hardly perhaps obtains in à Kempis the prominence which belongs to it in connexion with his subject. This is the doctrine of union with Christ, which may be called the other pole of St. Paul's system. St. Paul's whole teaching revolves between the two poles of righteousness through the death of Christ for us and holiness through the life of Christ in us. The latter truth is not absent from the pages of the *Imitation*; but its importance is not fully brought out.

For, beautiful as the phrase "the imitation of Christ" is, it hardly indicates the deepest way in which Christ's people become like Him. Imitation is rather an external process: it denotes the taking of that which is on one and putting it on another from the outside. But it is not chiefly by such an external copying that a Christian grows like Christ, but by an internal union with Him. If it is by a process of imitation at all, then it is imitation like that of a child copying its mother. This is the completest of imitations. The child reproduces the mother's tones, her gestures, the smallest peculiarities of her gait and movements, with an amazing and almost laughable perfection. But why is the imitation so perfect? It may be said it is because of the child's innumerable opportunities of seeing its mother, or because of the minuteness of a child's observation. But every one knows that there is more in it than this. The mother is in her child; at its birth she communicated her own nature to it; and it is to the working in the child of this mysterious influence that the success of the imitation is due. In like manner we may carefully copy the traits of Christ's character, looking at Him outside of us, as a painter looks at his model; we

---

* On this point see the singularly lofty and weighty statement of Martensen, On the Imitation of Christ and Justifying Faith, in his *Christian Ethics*, vol. i.

may do better still—we may, by prayer and the reading of the Word, live daily in His company, and receive the impress of His influence; but, if our imitation of Him is to be the deepest and most thorough, something more is necessary: He must be in us, as the mother is in her child, having communicated His own nature to us in the new birth.*

IV.

There is, however, a defect in the *Imitation* which the reader of to-day feels more than any of these: it lacks the historical sense, which is the guide of the modern mind in every kind of inquiry. Though the spirit of Christ pervades the book and many of its chapters are so full of the essence of His teaching that they might be appended as invaluable comments to His sayings, yet it presents no clear historical image of Him.

This would seem, however, to be the one thing needful for successful imitation. If we are to try to be like Christ, we must know what He was like. No painter could make a satisfactory copy of a figure of which he had himself only a vague conception. Yet no exact image of Christ will be found in à Kempis. To him Christ is the union and sum of all possible excellences; but he constructs Christ out of his own notions of excellence, instead of going to the records of His life and painting the portrait with the colours they supply. He specifies, indeed, certain great features of the Saviour's history—as, for instance, that in becoming man He humbled Himself, and therefore we ought to be humble; or that He lived a life of suffering, and therefore we ought to be willing to suffer; but he does not get beyond these generalities.

Now, it is possible to construct out of the Gospels a more lifelike portrait than this. It is possible at present as it has never been in any former age. Our century will be remembered in the history of Christian thought as the first which concentrated its attention

---

* "Christi Vorbild ist mehr als kahles, kaltes Tugendbeispiel, es ist erwärmende, erzündende Lebensgemeinschaft."—KÖGEL, *Predigten*, i. 86.

on the details of the Life of Christ. The works written on this subject in recent times have been without number, and they have
powerfully affected the mind of the age. The course of Christ's life
on earth has been traced from point to point with indefatigable
patience and illustrated with knowledge from every quarter; every
incident has been set in the clearest light; and we are now able
to follow Him as it has never been possible to do before into
every department of life—such as the family, the state, the
Church, the life of prayer, the life of friendship, and so on—and
to see exactly how He bore Himself in each. This is the method
of knowing Him which has been granted to our age; and to be
content to know Him merely as a vague image of all possible
excellences would be to us like painting a landscape in the stu-
dio from mere general conceptions of mountains, rivers and
fields, instead of going direct to nature.

Of course it is easy to exaggerate the value of a method.
Infinitely more important always are the mind and heart working
behind the method. The glowing love, the soaring reverence, the
range and sublimity of thought in à Kempis, have brought the
object home to him with a closeness and reality which fill every
sympathetic reader with a sacred envy and will always enchain
the Christian heart.* Yet, though an improved method is not
everything, it is something; and, if we feel our own devotion to
be cold, and the wing of our thought feeble in comparison with
others, all the more ought we to grasp at whatever advantage it
may be able to supply. The imitation of Christ is a subject which
is constantly calling for reconsideration; for the evolution of history and the progress of knowledge place people on new points
of view in relation to it. Each generation sees it in its own way,

---

* In reading the Psalms, who has not coveted the nearness to God which their
authors attained, and the splendid glow of feeling which contact with Him produced in them? Who has not questioned whether he has ever himself penetrat-
ed so far into the secret of the Lord? Yet this does not blind us to the superior
freedom and fulness of access to the divine presence allowed under the New
Testament.

and the last word on it can never be spoken. The historical method of handling it is the one which falls in with those habits of thought which have been worn into the mind of our age by its vast conquests in other directions; and, though it will not make up for the lack of faith and love, it is a *charisma* which the Church is bound to use, and on the use of which God will bestow His blessing.

V.

It can hardly be said that evangelical thought has hitherto claimed this subject cordially enough as its own. The evangelical heart, indeed, has always been true to it. I have sometimes even thought that among the causes of the popularity of à Kempis' book not the least potent is its mere name. The Imitation of Christ! the very sound of this phrase goes to the heart of every Christian and sets innumerable things moving and yearning in the soul. There is a summons in it like a ravishing voice calling us up sunny heights. It is the sum of all which in our best moments and in our deepest heart we desire.

But, whilst to Christian experience the imitation of Christ has always been inexpressibly precious, it has held, in evangelical preaching and literature, on the whole, only an equivocal position. The Moderatism which in last century nearly extinguished the religion of the country made much of the example of Christ. But it divorced it from His atonement, and urged men to follow Christ's example, without first making them acquainted with Him as the Saviour from sins that are past. The Evangelicals, in opposition to this, made Christ's atonement the burden of their testimony and when His example was mentioned, were ever ready with, Yes, but His death is more important. Thus it happened that the two parties divided the truth between them, the example of Christ being the doctrine of the one and His atoning death that of the other. In like manner, when Unitarianism seemed for a time, through the high character and splendid eloquence of Channing, to be about to become a power in the world, it derived nearly all the attractiveness it ever possessed from the eulogies in which its preaching abounded of the pure, lofty and self-sacrificing humanity of Christ. The evangelical Church answered with demonstrations of His divinity, scriptural and irresistibly logical no doubt, but not always very captivating. And thus a division was again allowed to take place, the humanity of Christ falling to the one party as its share and His divinity to the other.

It is time to object to these divisions. Both halves of the truth are ours, and we claim the whole of it. The death of Christ is ours, and we rest in it our hopes of acceptance with God in time and in eternity. This is what we begin with; but we do not end with it. We will go on from His death to His life and, with the love begotten of being redeemed, try to reproduce that life in our own. In the same way, whilst glorying in His divinity, we will allow none to rob us of the attraction and the example of His humanity; for, indeed, the perfection of His humanity, with what this implies as to the value of His testimony about Himself, is the strongest bulwark of our faith that He was more than man.

II.

Christ in the Home

Matt.	viii. 14, 15.
	ix. 18-26.
	xvii. 18.
	xviii. 1-6.
	xix. 13-15.
Mark	v. 18, 19.
	xii. 18-25.
Luke	vii. 11-15.
	xi. 27, 28.
John	viii. 1-11.
	xix. 25-27.
Matt.	xii. 46-50.
Luke	ix. 57-62.
Matt.	i.
	ii.
Luke	i. 26-56.
	ii.
	iii. 23-38.
Matt.	xiii. 55-58.
Luke	iv. 16, 22.
John	vi. 42.
Mark	iii. 21.
John	vii. 3-9.

CHAPTER II.

Christ in the Home.

I.

The institution of the family affords striking illustrations both of what may be called the element of necessity and of what may be called the element of liberty in human life.

There is in it a mysterious element of necessity. Everyone is born into a particular family, which has a history and character of its own, formed before he arrives. He has no choice in the matter; yet this connection affects all his subsequent life. He may be born where it is an honour to be born or, on the contrary, where it is a disgrace. He may be heir to inspiring memories and refined habits, or he may have to take up a hereditary burden of physical and moral disease. A man has no choice of his own father and mother, his brothers and sisters, his uncles and cousins; yet on these ties, which he can never unlock, may depend three-fourths of his happiness or misery. The door-bell rings some night, and, going out, you see on the doorstep a man who is evidently a stranger from a strange land. You know nothing of him; he is quite outside the circle of your interest; he is ten thousand miles away from your spirit. But, if he can say, "Don't you know me? I am your brother," how near he comes—ten thousand miles at one step! You and he are connected with an indissoluble bond; and this bond may either be a golden clasp which is an ornament or an iron clamp which burns and corrodes your very flesh. This is the element of necessity in the institution of the family.

Jesus could not touch humanity without being caught in this fetter of necessity. He entered its mysterious circle when He was born of a woman. He became a member of a family which had its own traditions and its own position in society; and He had brothers and sisters.

These circumstances were not without importance to Him. That His mother exercised an influence upon His growing mind cannot be doubted. We have not, indeed, the means of tracing in much detail how this influence acted, for few notices of His early years have come down to us; but it may be noted as one significant fact that Mary's hymn, the so-called Magnificat, in which, at her meeting with Elizabeth, she poured forth the sentiments of her heart, embodies thoughts which are echoed again and again in the preaching of Jesus. This production proves her to have been a woman not only of great grace, but of rare natural gifts, which had been nourished from God's Word, till she naturally spoke the very language of the prophets and the holy women of old. We may not ascribe too much to her and Joseph, but we can say that the holy childhood of Jesus was reared in a home of pious refinement, and that there were marks of this home on Him after He left it.

Besides this influence, He was born to a long pedigree; and this was not a matter of indifference to Him. He was of the seed of David; and the Gospel narrative takes pains to trace His descent in the royal line—a procedure which may be regarded as an echo of His own feeling. *Noblesse oblige*: there is a stimulus to noble action supplied by noble lineage; and Milton is not perhaps overstepping the bounds of legitimate inference when, in *Paradise Regained*, he represents the mind of the youthful Saviour as being stirred to noble ambition by the memories of His ancestors:

Victorious deeds
Flamed in My heart, heroic acts—one while
To rescue Israel from the Roman yoke;
Then to subdue and quell o'er all the earth
Brute violence and proud tyrannic power,
Till truth was freed and equity restored.

There can at least be no hesitation in believing that His royal descent pointed out His way to the work of the Messiah.

He had, however, also to feel the galling of the ring of necessity. He bore the reproach of mean descent; for, although His remoter ancestry was noble, His immediate relatives were poor; and, when He appeared on the stage of public life, sneering tongues asked, "Is not this the carpenter's son?" His life is the final rebuke to such shallow respect of persons, and will remain for ever to the despised and lowly-born a guide to show how, by worth of character and wealth of service to God and man, they may shut the mouths of gainsayers and win a place in the love and honour of the world.

The element of liberty which belongs to human life is exhibited no less conspicuously than the element of necessity in the family, and is equally mysterious. Of his own choice a man enters the married state and founds a family; and by this act of his will the circle is fashioned which in the next generation will be inclosing other human beings in the same bonds of relationship into which he has himself been born.

Of course the nature of the case prevented Jesus from being the founder of a family; and this has sometimes been pointed to as a defect in the example He has left us. We have not, it is said, His example to follow in the most sacred of all the relationships of life. Undeniably there seems to be a certain force in this objection. Yet it is a singular fact that the greatest of all precepts in regard to this relationship is taken directly from His example. The deepest and most sacred word ever uttered on the subject of marriage is this: "Husbands, love your wives, even as Christ also loved the Church, and gave Himself for it; that He might sanctify and cleanse it with the washing of water by the Word, that He might present it to Himself a glorious Church, not having spot, or wrinkle, or any such thing; but that it should be holy and without blemish."*

II.

Jesus honoured the institution of the family all through His life.

In His day there prevailed in Palestine a shameful dissolution of the domestic ties. Divorce was rife and so easily procured that every trifle was made an excuse for it; and by the system of Corban children were actually allowed to compound by a payment to the Temple for the neglect of their own parents. Jesus denounced these abuses with unsparing indignation and sanctioned for all the Christian ages only that law of marriage which causes it to be entered on with forethought,† and then, when the relationship has been formed, drains the deepest affections of the heart into its sacred channel.

His own love of children, and the divine words He spoke about them, if they cannot be said to have created the love of parents for their children, have at all events immensely deepened and refined it. The love of heathen mothers and fathers for their offspring is a rude and animal propensity in comparison with the love for children which reigns in our Christian homes. He lifted childhood up, as He raised so many other weak and despised things, and set it in the midst. If the patter of little feet on the stairs

---

* Eph. v. 25 ff.

† "He who attacks marriage, he who by word or deed sets himself to undermine this foundation of all moral society, he must settle the matter with me; and, if I don't bring him to reason, then I have nothing to do with him. Marriage is the beginning and the summit of all civilisation. It makes the savage mild; and the most highly cultivated man has no better means of demonstrating his mildness. Marriage must be indissoluble; for it brings so much general happiness, that any individual case of unhappiness that may be connected with it cannot come into account. . . . Are we not really married to our conscience, of which we might often be willing to rid ourselves because it often annoys us more than any man or woman can possibly annoy one another?"—BLACKIE, *The Wisdom of Goethe.*

and the sound of little voices in the house are music to us, and if the pressure of little fingers and the touches of little lips can make us thrill with gratitude and prayer, we owe this sunshine of life to Jesus Christ. By saying, "Suffer the little children to come unto Me," He converted the home into a church, and parents into His ministers; and it may be doubted whether He has not by this means won to Himself as many disciples in the course of the Christian ages as even by the institution of the Church itself. Perhaps the lessons of mothers speaking of Jesus, and the examples of Christian fathers, have done as much for the success of Christianity as the sermons of eloquent preachers or the worship of assembled congregations. Not once or twice, at all events, has the religion of Christ, when driven out of the Church, which had been turned by faithless ministers and worldly members into a synagogue of Satan, found an asylum in the home; and there have been few of the great teachers of Christendom who have not derived their deepest convictions from the impressions made by their earliest domestic environment.

Many of the miracles of Jesus seem to have been prompted by regard for the affections of the family. When He healed the Syro-Phœnician's daughter, or gave the daughter of Jairus back to her mother, or raised the widow's son at the gate of Nain, or brought Lazarus from the dead to keep the family circle at Bethany unbroken, can it be doubted that the Saviour experienced delight in ministering to the domestic affections? He showed how profound was His appreciation of the depth and intensity of these affections in the Parable of the Prodigal Son.

But it was by His own conduct in the family that He exhibited most fully His respect for this institution. Though the details of His life in Mary's home are unknown to us, every indication shows Him to have been a perfect son.

There is no joy of parents comparable to that of seeing their child growing up in wisdom, modesty and nobility; and we are told that Jesus grew in wisdom and stature and in favour with God and man. If He knew already of the great career before Him, this did not lift Him above the obedience of a child; for, even when He was twelve years of age, we are told, He went down to Nazareth with His parents and was subject unto them. It is generally supposed that soon after this Joseph died, and on Jesus, as the eldest son, fell the care of supporting the family. This is uncertain; but the very close of His life is marked by an act which throws the strongest light back on the years of which no record has been preserved, for it reveals how deep and deathless was His affection for His mother. Whilst hanging on the cross, He saw her and spoke to her. He was at the time in terrible agony, every nerve tingling with intolerable pain. He was at the point of death and anxious no doubt to turn away from all earthly things and deal with God alone; He was bearing the sin of the world, whose maddening load was crushing His heart; yet, amidst it all, He turned His attention to His mother and to her future, and made provision for her by asking one of His disciples to take her to his home and be a son to her in His own stead. And the disciple He selected for this service was the most amiable of them all—not Peter the headlong or Thomas the melancholy, but John, who could talk with her more tenderly than any other about the one subject which absorbed them both, and who was perhaps abler than any of the rest, on account of the comfort of his worldly condition, to support Mary without allowing her to feel that she was a burden.

III.

Sacred as is the parent's right to the obedience of the child, there is a term to it. It is the office of the parent to train the child to independence. As the schoolmaster's aim ought to be to train his pupils to a stage where they are able to face the work of life without any more help from him, so parents have to recognise that there is a point at which their commands must cease and their children be allowed to choose and act for themselves. Love will not cease; respect ought not to cease; but authority has to cease. Where exactly this point occurs in a child's life it is difficult to define. It may not be the same in every case. But in all cases it is a momentous crisis. Woe to the child who grasps at this freedom too soon! This is often the ruin of the young; and among the features of the life of our own time there are none perhaps more ominous than the widespread disposition among the young to slip the bridle of authority prematurely and acknowledge no law except their own will. But parents also sometimes make the mistake of attempting to exert their authority too long. A father may try to keep his son under his roof when it would be better for him to marry and have a house of his own; or a mother may interfere in the household affairs of her married daughter, who would be a better wife if left to her own resources.*

Mary, the mother of Jesus, erred in this respect. She attempted again and again to interfere unduly with His work, even after His public ministry had commenced. It was her pride in Him that made her do so at the marriage in Cana of Galilee; it was anxiety about His health on other occasions. She was not the only one who ventured to control His action in an undue way. But, if anything could arouse the indignation of Jesus, it was such interference. It made Him once turn on Peter with, "Get thee behind Me, Satan;" and on more than one occasion it lent an appearance of harshness even to His behaviour to His mother. The very intensity of His love to His friends and relatives made their wishes and appeals sore temptations to Him, for He would have liked to please them had He been able. But, if He had yielded, He would

---

* "A *child's* duty is to obey its parents. It is never said anywhere in the Bible, and never was yet said in any good or wise book, that a man's or a woman's is. *When*, precisely, a child becomes a man or a woman, it can no more be said, than when it should first stand on its legs. But a time assuredly comes when it should. In great states, children are always trying to remain children, and the parents wanting to make men and women of them. In vile states the children are always wanting to be men and women, and the parents to keep them children. It may be—and happy the house in which it is so—that the father's at least equal intellect, and older experience, may remain to the end of his life a law to his children, not of force, but of perfect guidance, with perfect love. Rarely it is so; not often possible. It is as natural for the old to be prejudiced as for the young to be presumptuous; and in the change of centuries, each generation has something to judge of for itself."—RUSKIN, *Mornings in Florence*, vol. iii., p. 72.

have been turning away from the task to which He was pledged; and therefore He had to rouse Himself even to indignation to resist temptation.

On no other occasion had His conduct so much appearance of unfilial harshness as when His mother and brethren came one day in the midst of His work desiring to speak with Him, and He retorted on the person who told Him, "But who is My mother, and who are My brethren?" and, looking round on the disciples seated in front of Him, added, "Behold, My mother and My brethren! for whosoever shall do the will of God, the same is My brother, and sister, and mother." It cannot be denied that these words have a harsh sound.* But they are probably to be read with what goes immediately before them in the Gospel of St. Mark, where we are told that His friends made an attempt to lay hold of Him, saying, "He is beside Himself." So absorbed was Jesus at this period in His work that He neglected even to eat; so rapt was He in the holy passion of saving men that to His relatives it appeared that He had gone mad; and they conceived it to be their duty to lay hands on Him and put Him in restraint. If Mary took part in this impious procedure, it is no wonder that there should have fallen on her a heavy rebuke. At all events she evidently came to Him thinking that He must at once leave everything and speak to her. But He had to teach her that there are even higher claims than those of domestic affection: in doing God's work He could recognise no authority but God's.

There is a sphere into which even parental authority may not seek admittance—the sphere of conscience. Jesus not only kept this sacred for Himself, but called upon those who followed Him to do so too. He foresaw how in the progress of time this would often sever family ties; and to one who cherished so high a respect for the home it must have been a prospect full of pain:

---

* The very fact, however, that Jesus compared the relation between Himself and those who do the will of God to the connection between Himself and His mother and brethren implies that the latter held a high and sacred place in His mind.

"Think not," He said, "that I am come to send peace on earth, but a sword. For I am come to set a man at variance against his father, and the daughter against her mother, and the daughter-in-law against her mother-in-law. And a man's foes shall be they of his own household." This must have been to Him a terrible prospect; but He did not shrink from it; to Him there were claims higher than even those of home: "He that loveth father and mother more than Me is not worthy of Me, and he that loveth son or daughter more than Me is not worthy of Me."

This sword still cuts. In heathen countries where Christianity is being introduced, especially in countries, like India, where the domestic system is extensively developed, the chief difficulty in the way of confessing Christ is the pain of breaking family connections, and often it is nothing less than an agony. Even in Christian lands the opposition of worldly parents to the religious decision of their children is sometimes very strong, and occasions extreme perplexity to those who have to bear this cross. It is always a delicate case, requiring the utmost Christian wisdom and patience; but, when the issues are clear to mind and conscience, there can be no doubt which alternative is the will of Christ: we must obey God rather than man.* How happy are they who are in precisely the opposite case: who know that their full decision for Christ and frank confession of Him would fill their homes with joy unspeakable!

IV.

In every home, it is said, there is a skeleton in the cupboard; that is to say, however great may be its prosperity and however perfect the appearance of harmony it presents to the world, there

---

* There is a very important caution hinted at in the words of Martensen on this subject (*Christian Ethics*, vol. ii.): "Whatever doubtful and difficult circumstances may hereby arise, and however mistakenly those members of a family may act, who are awake to Christian truth, but whose Christianity is often made an unseemly display of, and whose whole behaviour is one fret and ferment, still the fact itself, that *ordinary* and *worldly* family life is disturbed by the Gospel, is one quite in order, and in conformity with the divine economy."

is always, inside, some friction or fear, or secret, which darkens the sunshine.

This proverb may be no truer than many other wide generalisations which need to be qualified by the acknowledgment of innumerable exceptions. Yet there is no denying that home has its pains as well as its pleasures, and the very closeness of the connection of the members of a family with one another gives to any who may be so disposed the chance of wounding the rest. Under the cloak of relationship torture may be applied with impunity, which those who inflict it would not dare to apply to an outsider.

Jesus suffered from this: He had His peculiar domestic grief. It was that His brethren did not believe on Him. They could not believe that He who had grown up with them as one of themselves was infinitely greater than they. They looked with envy on His waxing fame. Whenever they intervene in His life, it is in a way to annoy.

How great a grief this must have been to Jesus will be best understood by those who have suffered the like themselves. There have been many of God's saints who have had to stand and testify alone in ungodly and worldly homes. Many in such circumstances are suffering an agony of daily petty martyrdom which may be harder to bear than public persecution, for which widespread sympathy is easily aroused. But they know at least that they have the sympathy of Him who alluded so pathetically to His own experience in the words: "A prophet is not without honour save in his own country and in his own house."

How He met His brethren's unbelief—whether He reasoned and remonstrated with them or was silent and trusted to the testimony of His life—we cannot tell. But we may be certain that He prayed for them without ceasing; and happily we know what the issue was.

His brethren, it would appear, continued unbelieving up to the time of His death. But immediately thereafter, in the first chapter of the Book of Acts, we find them assembled as believers with

His apostles in Jerusalem.* This is an extraordinary circumstance; for at this very time His cause was, if we may so speak, at the lowest ebb. Events seemed to have demonstrated that His pretensions to the Messiahship had been false; yet those who had disbelieved in Him at the height of His fame were found among the believers in Him when apparently His cause had gone to pieces. How is this to be accounted for?

The explanation lies, I believe, in a passage of First Corinthians, where, in enumerating the appearances of our Lord to different persons after His resurrection, St. Paul mentions that He appeared to James.† This was apparently the Lord's brother; and, if so, is there not something wonderfully striking in the fact that one of the first acts of the risen Saviour was to bring to His unbelieving brother the evidence which would conquer his unbelief? James, it may be presumed, would communicate what he had experienced to the other members of Mary's family. The result was of the happiest description; and two of the brothers, James and Jude, lived to be the penmen of books of Holy Scripture.

I venture to think that the presence of these brethren of Jesus among the believers in Him at such a crisis is even yet one of the strongest proofs of the reality of the resurrection; but in the meantime we will rather think of it as a signal proof of the unwearied persistence with which He sought their salvation, and as an example to ourselves to pray on, hope on, work on for those of our own flesh and blood who may yet be outside the fold of Christ.

---

* Acts i. 14.
† I Cor. xv. 7.

III.

Christ in the State

Matt.	ix. 1.
	xiii. 54.
	xvii. 24-27.
	xx. 17-19.
	xxiii. 37-39.
	xxvi. 32.
Luke	iv. 16-30.
	xiii. 16, 34, 35.
	xix. 9.
Matt.	ii.
	iv. 3-10.
	ix. 9, 27.
	xxi. 1-11.
	xxii. 15-21.
	xxvi. 47-68.
	xxvii.
Luke	ii. 11, 29, 32, 38.
	xiii. 31-33.
	xxiii. 7-12.
John	vi. 15.
	xi. 48.
Matt.	xviii. 1-3.
	xix. 28.
	xx. 20-28.
John	xviii. 36, 37.
	xix. 14, 19, 20.

CHAPTER III.

Christ in the State.

I.

In the mind of the average Christian of the present day the idea of the state does not perhaps occupy a prominent position. Many of his duties appear to him more important than those he owes as a citizen. He probably considers that the most important question which can be asked about him is, What is he in himself, in his secret soul and inward character? Next to this in importance he might perhaps consider the question of what he is as a member of the Church, charged with sustaining its honour and sharing in its work. The third place he might give to the question of what he is in the family, as son, husband, father. But much less important than any of these would appear to him the fourth question—what he is as a citizen of the state.

On the whole, perhaps this is the right way of judging; probably it is the Christian way.* But it is the exact opposite of the view of the whole ancient world. The great thinkers of Greece,

---

* The relative importance of these different ways of considering man affords scope, however, for endless discussion and difference of opinion. Rothe's ethical speculations were powerfully influenced by deference to the ancient view of the priority of the state. Martensen holds that a theory of society must start from the family. Ritschl and his school have re-emphasized the ethical and religious importance of the Church. Among ourselves several causes are contributing at present to give prominence to the social aspects of religion. It is impossible to

for example, put the state before the individual, the home and the Church. To them the supreme question about every man was, What is he as a citizen? The chief end of man they believed to be to make the state great and prosperous, and to the interests of the state they sacrificed everything else. Whether the individual was good and happy, whether the family was pure and harmonious, was not what they asked first, but whether the state was strong.

Jesus changed this. He was the discoverer, so to speak, of the individual. He taught that in every man there is a soul more precious than the whole world, and that the best product of this world is a good and noble character. Instead of its being true that individuals do not matter if the state is strong, the truth is that the state and the Church and the family are only means for the good of the individual, and they are tested by the kind of man they produce.* In this, as in many other respects, Christianity turned the world upside down, and put the first last and the last first.

But, although the state does not hold the place in Christian teaching which it held in heathen philosophy, it would be a great mistake to suppose that to Christianity the state is unimportant. Though the primary aim of Christ's religion is to make good men, yet good men ought to be good citizens.

II.

It is natural to a healthy human being to love the land of his birth, the scenery on which his eyes have first rested, and the town in which he resides; and it is part of the design of Providence to utilise these affections for the progress of man and the embellishment of the earth, which is his habitation. Every inhabitant of a town ought to wish to promote its welfare and

---

overestimate these, unless they are put above its individual aspects. I can entertain no doubt that in the mind of Jesus the individual was the *prius*. Indeed, one of the most decisive steps forward taken in His moral teaching was the substitution of the individual as the unit for the nation or the Church.

* "The test of every religious, political, or educational system is the man which it forms."—*Amiel's Journal*, vol. i., p. 49.

adorn it with beauty; and there is no feeling more worthy of a youthful heart than the desire to do something—by making a wise plan, or writing a good book, or singing a noble lay, or expunging a national blot—to add to the fair fame of his native country.*

Some countries have had an exceptional power of awakening these sentiments and of binding their own children to their service. Palestine was one of these. It was loved with a fervent patriotism. Its charm lay partly in its beauty. It may have lain partly in its very smallness, for feeling contracts an impetuous force when confined within narrow limits, as highland rivers become torrents in their rocky beds. But it is the memory of great and unselfish lives lived on its soil that chiefly excites patriotic sentiment in the inhabitants of any country;† and Palestine possessed this source of fascination in unparalleled measure, for its history was crowded with the most inspiring names.

Jesus felt this spell. Can any one read in His words the images of natural beauty gathered from the fields of Galilee without being convinced that He looked on these landscapes with a loving eye? The name of the village He was brought up in clings to Him to this day, for He is still Jesus of Nazareth. He vindicated Himself for healing a woman on the Sabbath on the ground that she was

---

* "I mind it weel, in early date,
When I was beardless, young and blate,
    And first could thresh the barn,

   *   *   *   *

Ev'n then a wish (I mind its power),
A wish that to my latest hour
    Shall strongly heave my breast:
That I for poor auld Scotland's sake
Some usefu' plan or beuk could make
    Or sing a sang at least"

                                  Burns

† Says Novalis: "The best of the French monarchs had it for his purpose to make his subjects so well off that every one of them should be able on Sundays to have roast fowl to dinner. Very good. But would not that be a better government under which the peasant would rather dine on dry bread than under any other on roast fowl, and, as grace before meat, would give God thanks that he had been born in such a country?"

a daughter of Abraham; and the publicans and sinners were dear to Him because they were the lost sheep of the house of Israel. Jerusalem, the capital of the country, had always laid a strong hold on Jewish hearts. The bards of the nation used to sing of it, "Beautiful for situation is Mount Zion;" "Let my tongue cleave to the roof of my mouth if I forget thee, O Jerusalem." But all such tributes of affection were surpassed by Jesus, when He addressed it, "O Jerusalem, Jerusalem, how often would I have gathered thy children together even as a hen gathereth her chickens under her wings!" This feeling survived even the transformation of the grave, for, in giving instructions, after He was risen, to His apostles about the evangelization of the world, He said, "Begin at Jerusalem." He lived in the closest sympathy with the great figures of His country's past and with the work done by them. Such names as Abraham and Moses, David and Isaiah, were continually on His lips; and He took up the tasks which they had left unfinished and carried them forward to their fulfilment. This is the truest work of patriotism. Happy is that country whose best life has been drained into some ideal cause, and whose greatest names are the names of those who have lavished their strength on this object. The deeds and sayings of these heroes ought, next to the Bible, to be the chief spiritual nourishment of her children; and the young ambition of her choicest minds should be concentrated on watering the seeds which they sowed and completing the enterprises which they inaugurated.

III.

There was one task of patriotism in Christ's day and country which seemed to lie to the hand of anyone born with a patriotic spirit. Palestine was at that time an enslaved country. In fact, it was groaning under a double servitude; for, whilst several of its provinces were ruled over by the tyrannical race of the Herods,* the whole country was subject to the Roman power.

---

* Herod the Great, the founder of this dynasty, was an Idumæan, but tried to conciliate the national sentiment by marrying a Jewish princess.

Was it not the duty of Jesus to free His country from this double tyranny and restore it to independence, or even elevate it to a place of sovereignty among the nations? Many would have been willing to welcome a deliverer and to make sacrifices for the national cause. The whole of the Pharisaic party was imbued with patriotic sentiment, and a section of it bore the name of the Zealots, because they were willing to go all lengths in sacrifice or daring.*

Jesus seemed to be designated for this very service. He was directly descended from David through the royal line. When He was born, wise men came from the East to Jerusalem inquiring, "Where is He that is born King of the Jews?" One of His first disciples,† on being introduced to Him, saluted Him as "the King of Israel;" and, on the day when He rode in triumph into Jerusalem, His adherents called Him by the same name, no doubt meaning that they expected Him to be literally the king of the country. These, and many other incidents which they will recall, are indications that it was His destiny not to be the private man He was, but to be the head of an emancipated and glorious state.

Why was this destination not fulfilled? This is the most difficult question that can be asked. It occurs often to every careful reader of the Gospels, but lands us as often as we ask it in a sea of mysteries. Did He ever intend to be the king of His native country? Was Satan appealing to the favourite fancies of His youth when he showed Him all the kingdoms of the world and the glory of them? If the Jewish people, instead of rejecting, had welcomed Him, what would have happened? Would He have set up His throne in Jerusalem and made the whole world subject to it? Was it only when they had made it impossible for Him to reign over them that He turned aside from what appeared to be His destiny and limited Himself to a kingdom not of this world?

---

* One member of this party, Simon Zelotes, joined the discipleship of Jesus.
† Nathanael.

It is impossible to read Christ's life intelligently without asking such questions as these; yet it is vain to ask them, for they cannot be answered. We are asking what would have been, if something which did happen had not happened; and only omniscience is equal to such a problem.

We may, however, say with certainty that it was the sin of man which prevented Jesus from ascending the throne of His father David. His offer of Himself to be the Messiah of His country was a *bonâ fide* offer. Yet it was made on conditions from which He could not depart: He could only have been king of a righteous nation. But the Jews were thoroughly unrighteous. They once tried to take Him by force and make Him a king; but their zeal was unhallowed, and He could not yield to it.

Then the tide of His life turned and rolled back upon itself. Instead of the expeller of tyrants, He became the victim of tyranny. His own nation, which ought to have raised Him on its shields as its leader, became His prosecutor at the bar of the alien government, and He had to stand as a culprit before both the Roman and the Herodian rulers of the land. As a subject of the country, He yielded with all submissiveness, telling His followers to put up their swords. And the law-officers of the state made a malefactor of Him, crucifying Him between two thieves. His blood fell on the capital of the country as a deadly curse; and in less than half a century after His murder the Jewish state had disappeared from the face of the earth.

It is a terrible commentary on the imperfection of the state. The state exists for the protection of life, property, and honour— to be a terror to evildoers and a praise to them that do well. Once, and only once in all history, it had to deal with One who was perfectly good; and what it did was to adjudge Him a place among the very worst of criminals and put Him to death. If this were a specimen of the law's habitual action, the state, instead of being a divine institution, would have to be pronounced the most monstrous evil with which the world is cursed. So the victims of its injustice have sometimes pronounced it; but happily such opinions are only the excesses of a few. On the whole, the laws framed by the state, and the administration of them, have been a restraint on sin and a protection to innocence. Yet the exceptions in every age have been numerous and sad enough. Not everything is righteous which the law of the land sanctions, nor are those all unrighteous whom the administrators of the law condemn. It is of the utmost consequence in our day to remember this, because, in the changed arrangements of the modern state, we are not only subjects of the government, but, directly or indirectly, makers and administrators of the law. Through the exercise of the municipal and the parliamentary franchises, we have a part in appointing those who make and who administer the laws, and thus we have our share in the responsibility of bringing up the laws to the standard of the divine justice and placing the wise and the good upon the judgment seat.

IV.

The life of Jesus appeared to miscarry. He who was meant to be a king was held unworthy to live even as a subject; instead of inhabiting a palace, He was consigned to a prison; instead of being seated on a throne, He was nailed to a tree.

But, although this was a miscarriage in so far as it was due to the wicked will of men, it was no miscarriage in the wisdom of God. Looked at from man's side, the death of Christ was the blackest spot on human history, a mistake and a crime without parallel; but, looked at from God's side, it is the grandest scene in the history of the universe; for in it human sin was expiated, the depths of the divine love were disclosed, and the path of perfection opened for the children of men. Jesus was never so completely a king as at the moment when His claims to kingship were turned into ridicule. It was in savage jest that the title was put above His cross, "This is Jesus, the King of the Jews." Pilate wrote these words in ridicule; but, when we look back at them now, do they appear ridiculous? Do they not rather shine across the centuries with inextinguishable splendour? In that hour of uttermost shame He was proving Himself to be the King of kings and the Lord of lords.

Jesus had all along had a conception of His own kingship which was distinct, original and often repeated. He held that to be a true king is to be the servant of the commonweal, and that he is most kingly who renders the most valuable services to the greatest number. He was well aware that this was not the world's view of kingship, but precisely the reverse of it. The world's view is that to be a king is to have multitudes in your service, and the greater the numbers ministering to his glory or pleasure the greater is the king. So He said "The princes of the Gentiles exercise dominion over them, and they that are great exercise authority upon them." "But," He added, "it shall not be so among you: but whosoever will be great among you, let him be your minister; and whosoever will be chief among you, let him be your servant." Such was Christ's conception of greatness; and, if it is the true one, He was never so great as when, by the sacrifice of Himself, He was conferring on the whole world the blessings of salvation.

But this conception of greatness and kingliness was not meant by Jesus to be applied to His own conduct alone; it is of universal application. It is the Christian standard for the measurement of all dignities in the state. He is greatest, according to the mind of Christ, who renders the greatest services to others.

Alas! this is as yet but little understood; it makes but slow progress in the minds of men. The old heathen idea is still the governing one of politics—that to be great is to receive much service, not to render it. Politics has been a game of ambition, if not a hunting-ground for rapacity, rather than a sphere of service. The aim of the governing classes hitherto has been to get as much as possible for themselves at the expense of the governed; and it has yet to be seen whether the new governing class is to be swayed by a better spirit.

Still, the Christian idea is growing in this department also of human affairs. The common heart responds to Christ's teaching, that the kingliest is he who sacrifices himself most willingly, works the hardest and achieves the most for the weal of all; and, although the quaint old saying of the Psalmist is still too true, that "men will praise thee when thou doest well to thyself," yet the number of those is daily growing who feel that the greatness of a ruler is measured, "not by the amount of tribute he levies on society, but by the greatness of the services he renders it."

IV.

Christ in the Church

Matt.	iii. 13-15.
	viii. 4.
	ix. 35.
	xiii. 54.
	xxi. 12, 13.
Mark	iii. 1-6.
	vi. 2.
	xii. 41-44.
Luke	ii. 21-24, 39, 41-49.
	iv. 16-32, 44.
	xxii. 53.
John	iv. 22.
	v. 1.
	viii. 20.
	x. 22, 23.

Matt.	ix. 10-17.
	xii. 1-14.
	xv. 1-9.
	xvi. 6.
	xxiii.
Luke	x. 31, 32.
John	ii. 13-22.

Matt.	xxiv. 1-2.
	xxvi. 17-30.
	xxviii. 19, 20.
John	xx. 22, 23.

CHAPTER IV.

Christ in the Church.

In some respects the Church is a narrower body than even the family; for one member of a family may be taken into it and another left out; but in other respects it is wider even than the state; for members of different nations may be members of the same Church.

The family and the state are institutions developed out of human nature by its own inherent force and according to its own inherent laws; but the Church is a divine institution, planted among men to gather into itself select souls and administer to them supernatural gifts. It is not, indeed, without a natural root in human nature; but this root consists of those feelings in man which make him aspire to an enjoyment and satisfaction which are not to be found in this world of which he is lord, but can only be got as the pure gift of Heaven. Without revelation there is no Church. As the edifice of the Church rises above the homes of men, amidst which it is erected, and its spire, like a finger, points to the sky, so the Church as an institution is an expression of man's aspirations after a heavenly life—a life in God and in eternity, which only the condescending grace of God can supply.

I.

Jesus was born in a country in which there was already a true Church, founded on revelation and administering the grace of

God. He was a child of that nation to which "pertained the adoption and the glory, and the covenants, and the giving of the law, and the service of God, and the promises." He was admitted into the fellowship of the Church by the ordinary gateway of circumcision; and a few weeks thereafter He was presented in the Temple, like any other Jewish child, in acknowledgment that He belonged to the Lord. Thus, before He was Himself conscious of it, He was, through the wishes of His earthly parents, shut in by holy rites within the visible Church of God.

In our day, all Christian parents devote their children to God; but too many of them show no disposition in maturity to desire for themselves to be connected with the house of God. Jesus, on the contrary, as soon as He became fully capable of self-conscious action, adopted the pious wishes of His parents as His own and developed a passionate love for the house of God. When His parents lost Him in Jerusalem at twelve years of age, they found Him again in the Temple; and, when they told Him how long and how widely they had sought Him, He asked in surprise how they could have expected Him to be anywhere else than there.* He was without a doubt a regular frequenter of the synagogue during His silent years at Nazareth; and strange it is to think of Him being preached to Sabbath after Sabbath for so long.†

When He quitted the privacy of Nazareth and began His public work, He was still a regular frequenter of the synagogue. This was in fact the centre from which His work developed itself. "He wrought miracles in the synagogues of Galilee." Nor was He neglectful of the other centre of Jewish worship—the Temple at

---

* "Wist ye not that I should be in My Father's house?" So the Revised Version, correctly.

† What was the man like who did it? Was he a wise man, who guided the footsteps of the Holy Child into the pastures of the Word and supplied Him with the language in which His own thoughts afterwards expressed themselves? or was he an embodiment of all that Jesus had afterwards to denounce in Pharisee and scribe? No portion of a congregation is more awe-inspiring to a minister than the children. Any Sunday there may be sitting before us one who is already revolving the thoughts which will dominate the future and supersede our own.

Jerusalem. He regularly attended the feasts; He sat down with His disciples in Jerusalem to eat the Passover; and He preached in the courts of the Temple. Even so secular a part of divine service as the giving of money He did not overlook: He sent Peter to fetch out of the fish's mouth a coin to pay for Him the Temple-tax; and He passed a glowing eulogium on the widow who cast her mite into the Temple collecting-box.

It is thus evident that Jesus was a passionate lover of the house of God. He could say with holy David, "How amiable are Thy tabernacles, O Lord of hosts; my soul longeth, yea, even fainteth for the courts of the Lord. A day in Thy courts is better than a thousand."

One sometimes hears even professedly religious people at the present day disparaging public worship, as if religion might flourish equally well without it; and, for trifling reasons or for no reason at all, they take it upon themselves to withdraw from the visible Church as something unworthy of them. This was not the way in which Jesus acted. The Church of His day was by no means a pure one; and He, if anybody, might have deemed it unworthy of Him. But He regularly waited on its ordinances and ardently loved it. There are few congregations less ideal perhaps than that in which He worshipped in wicked Nazareth, and few sermons are less perfect than those He listened to. But in that little synagogue He felt Himself made one with all the piety of the land; as the Scripture was read, the great and good of former ages thronged around Him; nay, heaven itself was in that narrow place for Him.

The Church is the window in the house of human life from which to look out and see heaven; and it does not require a very ornamental window to make the stars visible. The finest name ever given, outside the Bible, to the Church is Bunyan's Palace Beautiful. Yet the churches which he was acquainted with were only the Baptist meeting-houses of Bedfordshire; and in an age of persecution these were certainly as humble structures as have ever served for places of worship. No better than barns they seemed to common eyes; but in his eyes each of them was a Palace Beautiful; because, when seated on one of its rough benches, he felt himself in the general assembly and Church of the firstborn; and the eye of his imagination, looking up through the dingy rafters, could descry the gorgeous roof and shining pinnacles of the Church universal. It is the sanctified imagination that invests the Church building, whether it be brick meeting-house or noble cathedral, with true sublimity; and love to God, whose house it is, can make the humblest material structure a home of the spirit.

II.

Although the Church of Christ's day was of divine origin and He acknowledged it to be the house of God, it was frightfully full of abuses. Though an institution comes from God, man may add to it that which is his own; and by degrees the human addition may become so identified with the divine institution that both are supposed to be of a piece and equally divine. The human additions grow and grow, until it is almost impossible to get at what is God's through that which is man's. Some successful souls, indeed, still find their way through to the reality, as the roots of trees seek their way to the sustenance of the soil between the crannies of the opposing rocks; but multitudes are unable to find the way, and perish through trying to satisfy themselves with what is merely human, mistaking it for what is divine. At last a strong man is raised up to perceive the difference between the original structure and the human addition; and he tears away the latter, breaking it in pieces, amidst the wild outcries of all the owls and birds of darkness that have built their nests in it, and discloses once more the foundation of God. This is the Reformer.

In Christ's day the accumulation of human additions to the religion which God had instituted had grown to a head. No one knows how it had begun; such things sometimes begin innocently enough. But it had been immensely developed by a misconception which had crept in as to what the worship of God is. Worship is the means by which the empty human soul approaches God in order to be filled with His fulness, and then go away rejoicing, to live for Him in the strength thus received. But there is always a tendency to look upon it as a tribute we pay to God, which pleases Him and is meritorious on our part. Of course, if it is tribute paid to Him, the more of it that can be paid the better; for the more of it there is, so much the greater grows the merit of the worshipper. Thus services are multiplied, new forms are invented, and the memory of God's grace is lost in the achievements of human merit.

This was what had happened in Palestine. Religion had become an endless round of services, which were multiplied till they became a burden which life was unable to bear. The ministers of religion heaped them on the people, whose consciences were so crushed with the sense of shortcoming that the whole joy of religion was extinguished. Even the ministers of religion themselves were not able to perform all the orders they issued; and then hypocrisy came in; for naturally they were supposed to be doing those things which they prescribed to others. But they said and did not; they bound heavy burdens and grievous to be borne on other men's shoulders, while they themselves would not touch them with one of their fingers. It was high time for a reformer to appear, and the work fell to Jesus.

The first outburst of His reformatory zeal was at the outset of His ministry, when He drove the buyers and sellers out of the Temple. Their practices had probably commenced with good intentions: they sold oxen and doves for sacrifice to the worshippers from foreign countries, who came in tens of thousands to Jerusalem at the feast and could not easily bring these animals with them; and they exchanged the coins of Jerusalem for those of foreign countries, in which the strangers of course had brought their money. It was a necessary thing; but it had grown to be a vast abuse; for exorbitant prices were charged for the animals and exorbitant rates of exchange demanded; the traffic was carried on with such din and clamour as to disturb the worship; and it took up so much room that the Gentiles were elbowed out of the court of the Temple which belonged to them. In short, the house of prayer had become a den of thieves. Jesus had no doubt noted the abuse with holy anger many a time when visiting the Temple at the feasts; and, when the prophetic spirit descended on Him and His public ministry began, it was among His first acts to clear it out of the house of God. The youthful Prophet, with His scourge of cords, flaming above the venal crowd, that, conscious of their sin, fled, amidst tumbling tables and fleeing animals, from before His holy ire, is a perfect picture of the Reformer.

It is said that the high-priestly families derived an income from this unholy traffic, and it is not likely that they felt very kindly to One who thus invaded their vested interests. In like manner He aroused the resentment of the Pharisaic party by turning into ridicule their long and pretentious prayers and the trumpets they blew before them when they were giving alms. He could not but expose these practices, for the people had learned to revere as the flower of piety that which was the base weed of vulgarity and pride. He had to consent to be frowned upon as a man of sin because He neglected the fasts and the Sabbatic extravagances which He knew to be no part of religion; and still more because He mingled with publicans and sinners, though He knew this to be the very course of divine mercy. He was compelled at last to pluck the cloak of hypocrisy entirely away from the religious characters of the day and expose them in their true colours as blind leaders of the blind and whited sepulchres, which appeared fair outside, but inwardly were full of dead men's bones.

Thus He cleared away the human additions piled about the house of God and let the true Temple once more be seen in its own fair proportions. But He had to pay the penalty. The priests, the stream of whose sinful gains He had stopped, and the Pharisees, whose hypocrisy He had exposed, pursued Him with hatred that never rested till they saw Him on the cross. And so, in addition to the name of reformer, He earned the name of Martyr, and Himself became the leader of the noble army of martyrs which in a thin line deploys through the centuries.

Not a few of that army have also been reformers. They have risen against the abuses of the Church of their day and perished in the attempt. For the New Testament Church is no more free than was the Old Testament Church from the danger of being a scene of abuses. The condition of the Christian Church at the time of those men of God to whom we are wont specially to apply the title of the Reformers was remarkably like the state of the Old Testament Church in the time of Christ: man's additions had completely overlaid God's handiwork; religion had been transformed from an institution for the administration of God's grace into a round of forms and ceremonies for procuring God's favour by human merit; and the ministers of religion had become blind leaders of the blind. By the Reformation God delivered His Church from this state of things; and never since, we may hope, has there been anything like the same need of reform. It would be vain, however, to suppose that in our time or in the section of the Church to which we may belong there are no abuses needing the reformer's fan. Though we may be insensible of them, this is no proof that they do not exist; for the Church even in its worst days has been unconscious of its own defects, till the proper man has appeared and pointed them out; and in all ages there have been those who have believed themselves to be doing God service when resisting the most necessary changes.*

---

* Schism is the caricature of Reform. But Schismatic is often merely a nickname given to the true Reformer; and even real schism nearly always indicates the need for reform, as Schleiermacher has proved in the profound discussion of Church Reform in his *Christliche Sitte.* He says:

"Um also nichtigen Versuchen zu wehren, bedarf es zuvörderst der Unterweisung zu richtigem Schriftverständnisse, und dann muss auch immer das Bewusstsein erweckt werden, dass ein völliges Verstehen der Schrift nicht anders möglich ist, als auf dem Wege der gelehrten Bildung. Wäre in beider Hinsicht immer besser gesorgt gewesen, so würden viele Abnormitäten nicht entstanden sein. Dazu kommt aber noch etwas anderes. Es tritt nämlich nur zu oft der Fall ein, dass die Ehrfurcht, welche die Laien haben für die Wissenden als solche und für die Kirchenrepräsentation als Amt, gänzlich wieder aufgehoben wird durch die geringe persönliche Ehrfurcht, welche die Mitglieder der Repräsentation und

III.

The name Reformer, where it is truly deserved, is a great one in the Church; but to Jesus belongs one much greater; for He was the Founder of the Church.

The old Church in which He was brought up was ready to vanish away. It had served its day and was about to be taken down. He Himself prophesied that of the Temple there would soon not be left one stone above another; He told the woman of Samaria that the hour was coming when they would neither in Gerizim nor yet on Mount Zion worship the Father, but the true worshippers everywhere would worship Him in spirit and in truth; and, when He died, the veil of the Temple was rent in twain from the top to the bottom.

He founded the Church of the New Testament in His own blood. By the shedding of His blood He abolished the imperfect relation between God and men mediated by the blood of bulls and of goats, and established a new and better relationship. So He said in instituting the Lord's Supper, "This is the new covenant in My blood." The new house of God is illuminated with the perfect revelation made by Him of the Father; and in it are administered the new and richer blessings purchased by His life and death.

But in building the new house of God its Founder did not wholly discard the materials of the old.* He instituted the Lord's Supper in the very elements with which on the evening of its insti-

---

in welchen sonst das geschichtliche Leben ist einflössen. Wie sollte auch der Laie beides vereinigen, auf der einen Seite sich über jenen wissen in Beziehung auf Sittlichkeit und religiöse Kraft, und auf der anderen Seite sich ihrer höheren Erkenntniss unterordnen. Der geistliche Hochmuth würde also in den einzelnen nicht entstehen, wenn er nicht immer Vorschub fände einerseits in der Unvollkommenheit der Organisation, und andererseits darin, dass nicht Anstalten genug getroffen sind zur Verbreitung des richtigen Schriftverständnisses, und die Menge jener verkehrten Versuche in unserer Kirche ist ein sicheres Thermometer für den Zustand des ganzen in dieser Hinsicht. Wir werden auch des Uebels nicht Herr werden, ehe die Gründe desselben gehoben sind."

* The apparent contradiction between speaking of Christ both as the Reformer of the old and the Founder of the new is partly due to the contradiction, expounded in the preceding chapter, between the will of God and the will

tution He and His disciples were celebrating the Passover. The forms of worship and office-bearers of the Christian Church bear a close resemblance to those of the synagogue. Above all, the Scriptures of the Old Testament, with the figures of their saints and heroes, form part of the same volume as the Scriptures of the New.

Jesus Himself did not draw out in detail the plan of the New Testament Church. He contented Himself with laying its foundation, which none else could have done, and sketching the great outlines of its structure. He entrusted to it His Gospel, with the sacred charge to preach it to every creature; He gave to it the twelve apostles, whose labours and inspired teachings might serve as the second course of foundation-stones laid above the foundation which He had laid Himself; He empowered its officers to admit to, and exclude from, its fellowship; He instituted the sacraments of baptism and the Lord's Supper; and, above all, He left with His Church the promise, which is her star of hope in every age: "Lo, I am with you always, even to the end of the world."

This foundation-laying work of Christ was done once for all and cannot be repeated. Men dream sometimes of the Christian Church passing away and something more advanced taking its place. But "other foundation can no man lay." Only the building up of the Church on this foundation is now left to us. This, however, is part of the same work and may be done in the same spirit in which He laid the foundations.

In the first place, those who undertake it require to see to it that they build straight on the foundation. There is much that

---

of man. To finite eyes it cannot but seem that He was striving earnestly for ends which were not realised, and that the results of His life were different from His intentions. Besides, *old* and *new* are terms which may both be applicable to the same object at the same time. It is more orthodox to speak of the Christian Church as the same with that of the Old Testament; but it is perhaps more scriptural to speak of it as a new Church. That is to say, orthodoxy emphasizes the element which is common to both dispensations, whilst Scripture emphasizes what is distinctive in the new.

passes for Christian work that will not in the end be acknowledged by Christ, because it is not building on the foundation which He has laid. If that new covenant in His blood be ignored in which He declared His own work to consist, or if the foundations laid by His apostles in His name are not recognised, we may build a church of our own, but He will not recognise our labour.

All who take part in this work ought to build with His holy ardour. He thought it worth while to die for the sake of redeeming the souls of men; what sacrifices are we prepared to make in contributing to the same end? He gave His life; will we give up our ease, our effort, our money? It was because He believed every single soul was more precious than a world that He died to save the souls of men. Are they precious in our eyes? Does their fate haunt us? does their sin grieve us? would their salvation fill us with aught of the joy that thrills the angels in heaven when one sinner is converted?*

There is needed, however, not only zeal, but consecrated originality as well, in building this edifice. As I said, Jesus did not prescribe the minute details of the organization of the Church. He largely left it to human ingenuity to find out how best His work may be done; and the Church is only finding out still. New problems arise for her to solve, new tasks to be performed, and therefore she needs inventors and pioneers to devise the plans for her new enterprises and open up the way to new conquests. It is impossible, for example, to measure the blessing which that man conferred on the Church who instituted Sabbath schools. He was no dignitary of the Church nor perhaps in any way a remarkable man, except in this—that he saw a vast work needing to be done and had originality to discover the best way of doing it. He led

---

* "Christianity would sacrifice its divinity if it abandoned its missionary character and became a mere educational institution. Surely this Article of Conversion is the true *articulus stantis aut cadentis ecclesiæ.* When the power of reclaiming the lost dies out of the Church, it ceases to be the Church. It may remain a useful institution, though it is most likely to become an immoral and mischievous one. Where the power remains, there, whatever is wanting, it may still be said that 'the tabernacle of God is with men.'"—*Ecce Homo.*

the way into the children's world, and ever since he has been supplying the best of work for the myriads of willing reapers who
have followed him into that most attractive portion of the harvest-
field. There are plenty of other tasks awaiting solution from sanctified Christian genius; and I know no prize more to be coveted
than that of being the first to show how Christian thought may
exploit some new mine of spiritual knowledge, or Christian character rise to a new level of spiritual attainment, or Christian zeal
reach the spiritual wants of some neglected section of the community.

V.

Christ as a Friend

Matt.	x. 2-4.
	xi. 7-11.
	xvii. 1, 2.
	xviii. 6-10.
	xxi. 17.
	xxvi. 14-16, 37, 38, 40, 50.
	xxvii. 3-5, 55-61.
Mark	v. 37.
	xiii. 3, 4.
Luke	viii. 1-3.
	x. 38-42.
	xii. 4.
John	i. 35-51.
	xi.
	xii. 1-7.
	xiii. 1-5, 23.
	xv. 13-15.
	xix. 27.

CHAPTER V.

Christ as a Friend.

I.

It has been advanced as an objection to the New Testament that it never recommends friendship, and, while supplying rules for the behaviour to one another of husbands and wives, parents and children, brothers and sisters, gives none for the intercourse of friend with friend.*

Various reasons have been suggested to account for this singular omission. But, before entering upon these, it would be well to make sure that the omission itself is a reality. Is it true that the New Testament omits all reference to friendship?

I venture, on the contrary, to affirm that the New Testament is the classical place for the study of this subject. The highest of all examples of friendship is to be found in Jesus; and His behaviour

---

* In an argument designed to prove that Christianity is unfavourable to friendship, the fact might be adduced, that the best book on the subject is from the pen of a heathen. From the classical age of English theology we have two treatises on the subject, one from the Royalist side by Jeremy Taylor, the other from the Puritan side by Richard Baxter; but neither possesses the exquisite flavour of Cicero's *De Amicitiâ*. The *Lysis* of Plato is interesting, as opening some of the difficulties of the subject, but it is not an important dialogue. Shakspeare also has discussed some of the difficulties in *Two Noble Kinsmen* and *Two Gentlemen of Verona*, and he has given the whole subject an exquisite embodiment in *The Merchant of Venice*. But the glory of English literature in this department is *In Memoriam*.

in this beautiful relationship is the very mirror in which all true friendship must see and measure itself.

It is objected, indeed, that this instance is inadmissible, because Jesus sustained to those who may be called His friends the higher relationship of Saviour; and between those standing on such different levels, it is contended, real friendship was impossible.

But He Himself called the Twelve His friends: "Henceforth I call you not servants, but friends." From among the Twelve He made special companions of three—Peter, James and John; and of these three John was specially the disciple whom Jesus loved. We are told that "Jesus loved Martha and her sister and Lazarus;" and this notice surely implies that He stood in an attitude of peculiar friendliness towards the members of the family of Bethany. Merely as the Saviour, He is hardly to be thought of as loving one of those He has saved more than another; He loves them all alike. But in the cases just quoted He showed preferences for some of His followers over others; and this seems to prove that within the wider and higher relationship between Saviour and saved there was scope for the strictly human tie of friendship.

II.

Among those who have written on the subject of friendship it has been discussed whether the best friend is he who loves most or he who bestows the greatest benefits.

Much may be said on both sides; for, on the one hand, there is an infinite solace in the sincere affection of even the humblest friend, however unable he may be to render any material service; and, on the other hand, in the perplexities and misfortunes of life, which come to all, it is an unspeakable advantage to have one with a sound judgment and a helpful hand, who will interest himself in our affairs as if they were his own, because he is our friend. Yet I venture to think that neither of these is the pearl of friendship; there is something in it more valuable than either.

Let any one who has drunk deeply of this wellspring of happiness look back and ask what has been the sweetest ingredient in it: let him recall the friend of his heart, whose image is associated with the choicest hours of his experience; and then let him say what is the secret and the soul of his satisfaction. If your friendship has been of a high order, the soul of it is simply the worth of him you are allowed to call your friend. He is genuine to the core; you know him through and through, and nowhere is there any twist or doubleness or guile. It may be a false and disappointing world, but you have known at least one heart that has never deceived you; and, amidst much that may have happened to lower your estimate of mankind, the image of your friend has enabled you always to believe in human nature. Surely this is the incomparable gain of friendship—fellowship with a simple, pure and lofty soul.

If it is, what must have been the charm of the friendship of Jesus! If even the comparatively common and imperfect specimens of human nature we have known can make impressions so delightful, what must it have been to see closely that heart which was always beating with the purest love to God and man, that mind which was a copious and ever-springing fountain of such thoughts as have been preserved to us in the Gospels, that character in which the minutest investigation has never detected a single spot or wrinkle! As we read the records of the great and good, we cannot help sometimes wishing it had been our lot to follow Plato in his garden, or to hear the table-talk of Luther, or to sit with Bunyan in the sunshine of the streets of Bedford, or to listen to Coleridge bodying forth the golden clouds of his philosophy. But what would any such privilege have been in comparison with that of Mary,* who sat at Jesus' feet and heard His words;

---

* The heathen held woman to be unfit for this relationship, and too many Christian thinkers have followed in their footsteps, alleging such pleas as that a woman cannot keep a secret or that she cannot give counsel in affairs of difficulty. But Jesus "loved Martha and her sister;" some of His friends were women. Thus He vindicated the right of women to this honourable position, and

or that of John, who leant on His bosom and listened to the beating of His heart?

III.

If that which has just been mentioned is the prime excellence of friendship, love holds in it the second place.

Friendship is not the mere claim which one man may make on another because he was born in the same village or sat on the same bench at school; it is not the acquaintance of neighbours who have learned to like one another by daily gossiping from door to door, but would, if separated, forget one another in a month; it is not the tryst of roysterers, or the chance acquaintance of fellow-travellers, or the association of the members of a political party.* In real friendship there is always the knitting of soul to soul, the exchange of heart for heart. In the classical instance of friendship in the Old Testament, its inception is exquisitely described: "And it came to pass, when he had made an end of speaking unto Saul, that the soul of Jonathan was knit with the soul of David, and Jonathan loved him as his own soul." A union like this is formed not to be broken, and, if it is broken, it can only be with the tearing of the flesh and the loss of much blood.

---

hundreds of the best and manliest of His servants have since experienced the solace and strength springing from the friendship of good women; and, as one of them (Jeremy Taylor) has said, "a woman can love as passionately, and converse as pleasantly, and retain a secret as faithfully, and be useful in her proper ministries; and she can die for her friend as well as any Roman knight."

* "Zu trauter Freundschaft ist es nicht genug,
Dass man auf Du und Du ein Glas geleert,
Auf Einer Schulbank bei einander sass,
Zu trauter Freundschaft ist es nicht genug,
In Einem Café oft zusammentraf,
Sich auf der Strasse höflich unterhielt,
Im selben Club dieselben Lieder sang,
Als Publicisten Eine Farbe trug,
Auch in der Presse sich einander pries."
BAGGESEN, quoted by Martensen.

I cannot, however, agree with those who maintain that true friendship, like wedded love, can have but one object at a time. One of the finest spirits of our century, a thinker conversant with all the heights and depths of man's relationships with man,* has argued strongly in favour of this position, and he silences all objectors by replying that, if you think you have more friends than one, this only proves that you have not yet found the true one. But this is to misinterpret the nature of this affection, and force on it a rule belonging to quite a different passion. At all events, the example of Christ appears to support this view, and to prove that in friendship there may be different degrees, and that the heart is capable of enjoying several friendships at the same time.

IV.

The love of friends is an active passion, and delights in rendering services and bestowing benefits.

So sensible of this were the ancients that, in discussing the duties of friendship, what they asked was, not how much one friend ought to do for another, but where the limit was at which he ought to stop. They took it for granted that he would do, suffer and give all he could for his friend's sake; and they only prescribed to him to restrain himself at the point where his zeal might clash with some still higher obligation to his family, his country or his God. In accordance with this they represented friendship in art as a young man bare-headed and rudely attired, to signify activity and aptness for service. Upon the fringe of his garment was written *Death and Life*, as signifying that in life and death friendship is the same. On his forehead was inscribed *Summer and Winter*, meaning that in prosperity or adversity friendship knows no change except in the variety of its services. The left shoulder

---

* ROTHE. See his *Ethik*, vol. iv., p. 67. Germany is fortunate in having such examples of friendship among its greatest men as that of Luther and Melanchthon, and that of Goethe and Schiller.

and the arm were naked down to the heart, to which the finger of the right hand pointed at the words *Far and Near*, which expressed that true friendship is not impaired by time or dissolved by distance.*

Of this feature in the friendships of Jesus it would be easy to give examples; but none could be more striking than His behaviour at the death and resurrection of Lazarus. Every step of His on this occasion is characteristic. His abiding two days still in the place where He was, after receiving the news of His friend's death, in order to make the gift He was about to bestow more valuable; His venturing into Judæa in spite of the dangers He was exposed to and the fears of the Twelve; His fanning into flame of Martha's weak faith; His secret sending for Mary, that she might not miss the great spectacle; His sympathy with the emotions of the scene, so intense that He wept and the spectators exclaimed, "Behold, how He loved him;" His preparation of the sisters, by His prayer, for the shock of seeing their brother emerging from the sepulchre in his graveclothes; and then the benefaction of his resurrection—all these are traits of a love that was delicate as a woman's heart, strong as death and bountiful as heaven.

But friendship can sometimes show its strength as much by the readiness with which it accepts benefits as by the freedom with which it gives them. It proves by this its confidence in the love on the other side. Jesus gave such a proof of the depth of His friendship for John when, hanging on the cross, He asked the beloved disciple to adopt Mary as his own mother. Never was there a more delicate expression given to friendship. Jesus did not ask him if he would; He took his devotion for granted; and this trust was the greatest honour that could have been conferred on the disciple.

---

* From Jeremy Taylor's treatise on *Friendship*

V.

It Is a well-known characteristic of friendship that friends enjoy being in each other's company and hearing each other talk, and that they admit one another to the knowledge of secrets which they would not reveal to the world at large.

It is the commonest saying about two very intimate friends, that if you are seeking the one, you will do best to resort to the abode of the other. In each other's company they are at peace; speech between them is hardly necessary, for they have a subtler way of divining thought and feeling, and it is a precious privilege of friends to be silent in each other's company without awkwardness. Yet, when the gates of speech are opened, there is an outpouring of the mind's wealth such as takes place in no other circumstances. For nothing needs to be concealed. The shy thought, which scarcely ventured to show its face even to its own creator, is tempted out; the hardy opinion utters itself without fear; confidence is responded to with confidence; like two coals, burning feebly apart, which, when flung together, make a merry blaze, so mind and mind burn as they touch, and emit splendours which nothing but this contact could evoke. He is ignorant of one of the most glorious prerogatives of manhood who does not carry, treasured in his mind, the recollection of such golden hours of the feast of reason and the flow of soul.

Jesus expressly chose the Twelve "that they might be with Him." For three years they were His constant companions; and often He would take them away into uninhabited spots or on distant journeys for the express purpose of enjoying with them more uninterrupted intercourse. In the Gospel of St. John we have notes of these conversations, and from the wide contrast between the sayings of Jesus in this Gospel and those reported in the Synoptists, which rather represent His addresses to the people at large, we may perceive how fully in these interviews He opened to the Twelve His secret mind. And the kind of impressions which they received from these confidences may be learned from the saying of the two with whom He conversed on the way to Emmaus: "Did not our heart burn within us as He talked with us by the way, and as He opened to us the Scriptures?"

The minds of the most favoured apostles especially carried in subsequent years the priceless memory of many great hours like this, when, with hearts lost in wonder, they gazed into the vast and mystic realm of the thoughts of Christ. And they were vouchsafed a few hours even greater, when He took them away with Him to pray; as He did, for instance, when they beheld His glory in the Holy Mount, or when He invited them to watch with Him in Gethsemane. Never surely was He so unmistakably the human friend as when, on the latter occasion, He threw Himself on their sympathy, entreating them to be near Him in His agony.

These scenes excite our wonder that any should have been admitted so far into His secret life. Were not these hours of prayer especially too sacred for any mortal eyes to see? That His friends were admitted to them proves that it is a prerogative of friendship to be admitted far into the secrets of religious experience.

It is a truncated and most imperfect friendship when the gateway of this region is closed; for it means that the one friend is excluded from the most important province of the other's life. Hence it may be affirmed that friendship in its highest sense can exist only between Christians;* and even they only taste the bloom on this cup when they have arrived at the stage of free and frequent converse on those themes which were native to the mouth of Christ.

---

* "Ihre höchste Intensität hat die Freundschaft als religiöse Freundschaft, als Wahlanziehung der Freunde vermöge der specifischen Wahlverwandtschaft ihrer religiösen Individualitäten. Denn wegen der wesentlich centralen Stellung der Frömmigkeit im Menschen ist die religiöse specifische Sympathie der Individuen wesentlich specifische Sympathie derselben nach der Totalität ihrer sittlichen Individualität, nach dem ganzen innersten Kern derselben." ROTHE, *Christliche Ethik*, vol. iv., p. 68.

VI.

Friendship, like everything else, is tested by results. If you wish to know the value of any friendship, you must ask what it has done for you and what it has made you.

The friendship of Jesus could stand this test. Look at the Twelve! Consider what they were before they knew Him, and think what His influence made them and what position they occupy now! They were humble men, some of them, perhaps, with unusual natural gifts, but rude and undeveloped everyone. Without Him they would never have been anything. They would have lived and died in the obscurity of their peasant occupations and been laid in unmarked graves by the blue waters of the Sea of Galilee. They would never have been heard of twenty miles from home, and would all have been forgotten in less than a century. But His intercourse and conversation raised them to a place among the best and wisest of the sons of men; and they now sit on thrones, ruling the modern world with their ideas and example.

Our friendships, too, must submit to this test. There are friendships so called which are like millstones dragging down those who are tied to them into degradation and shame. But true friendship purifies and exalts. A friend may be a second conscience. The consciousness of what he expects from us may be a spur to high endeavour. The mere memory that he exists, though it be at a distance, may stifle unworthy thoughts and prevent unworthy actions. Even when the fear of facing our own conscience might not be strong enough to restrain us from evil, the knowledge that our conduct will have to encounter his judgment will make the commission of what is base intolerable.

Among the privileges of friendship one of the most valuable is the right of being told our faults by our friend. There are ridiculous traits of character in every man which all eyes see except his own; and there are dangers to character which the eye of a friend can discern long before they are visible to ourselves. It requires some tact to administer such reproof, and it requires some grace to take it gratefully; but "faithful are the wounds of a friend," and there are few gifts of friendship more highly to be prized than words of wise correction.*

Whilst, however, we estimate the value of the friendships we enjoy by their influence on us, it is no less important to remember that our own conduct in this relationship has to stand the same test. Is it good for my friend that I am his friend? In the maturity of his fully-formed judgment will he look back on the connection with approval? At the judgment-seat and in eternity will he prize it? A man will hesitate to answer these questions; but surely there is no object worthier of intense desire and earnest prayer than that our friendship may never be detrimental to him we love—that it may never pull him down, but help to raise and sustain him. Would it not be a prize better than any earthly distinction, if in the distant years, when we are old and grey-headed, or perhaps beneath the sod, there were one or two who could say, "His influence was a redeeming element in my life; he made me believe in goodness and think highly of human nature; and I thank God I ever knew him?"

There is no way in which we can have any guarantee of exerting such an influence except by keeping ourselves in contact with the great source of good influence. Christ was the friend of Peter and John and James, of Martha and Mary and Lazarus, in Palestine long ago. But He is still the friend of men; and, if we wish it, He will be ours. There are those who walk with Him and talk with

---

* Cicero adds something more: "Ut igitur et monere et moneri proprium est veræ amicitiæ, et alterum libere facere, non aspere, alterum patienter accipere, non repugnanter; sic habendum est, nullam in amicitiis pestem esse majorem, quam adulationem, blanditiam, assentationem: multis enim nominibus est hoc vitium notandum levium hominum atquo fallacium, ad voluntatem loquentium omnia, nihil ad veritatem. Cum autem omnium rerum simulatio vitiosa est (tollit enim judicium veri idque adulterat), tum amicitiæ repugnat maxime: delet enim veritatem, sine qua nomen amicitiæ valere non potest. Nam cum amicitiæ vis sit in eo, ut unus quasi animus fiat ex pluribus, qui id fieri poterit, si ne in uno quidem quoque unus animus erit idemque semper, sed varius, commutabilis, multiplex? Quid enim potest esse tam flexibile tam devium, quam animus eius qui ad alterius non modo sensum ac voluntatem, sed etiam vultum atque nutum convertitur?"—*De Amicitid*, cap. 25.

Him. They meet Him in the morning when they awake; He is with them in the street and at their work; they tell Him their secrets and appeal to Him in every time of need; they know Him better than any other friend. And these are they who have found the secret of existence and keep alive the faith of mankind in the reality of the life of Christ.

VI.

Christ in Society

Matt.	xi. 16-19.
Luke	xv. 1, 2.
	xix. 5-7.
	xxiv. 41-43.
Luke	xi. 37-44.
	xiv. 1-24.
Matt.	xxvi. 6-13.
Luke	vii. 36-50.
John	ii. 1-11.
	xii. 1-8.
Matt.	xiv. 15-21.
	xxvi. 26-30.
Luke	xxiv. 29-31.
John	xiii. 1-15.

CHAPTER VI.

Christ in Society.

Beyond the narrow circle of those whom we properly call our friends, there is a large circle of acquaintances, brought into connection with us in various ways, which may be designated by the vague term Society. Our intercourse with those to whom we are thus related raises questions which are not free from difficulty, but they receive light from the study of the conduct of Jesus.

I.

In this relationship there was a remarkable contrast between our Lord and His forerunner, the Baptist. John shunned society, living in the desert far from the abodes of men. His clothing was unsuited for the house or the town, and he confined himself to the ascetic fare of a hermit. The Saviour, on the contrary, descended among His fellowmen. Instead of waiting, like the Baptist, till people went out to Him, He came to them. In village and city, in street and marketplace, in synagogue and Temple—wherever two or three were gathered together, there was He in the midst of them. He entered beneath men's roofs, to rejoice with them when they were rejoicing and to weep with them when they wept. It is astonishing how often we read of His being at feasts. He began His ministry by attending a wedding. Matthew made Him a feast, and He went and sat down among the publican's motley guests. He invited Himself to the house of Zacchæus, another publican. Indeed, His eating with this class of persons came to be notorious.

But, when people from the other end of the social scale invited Him, He accepted their hospitality with equal readiness and sat down as frankly with scribes and Pharisees as among publicans and sinners. St. Luke mentions at least three occasions when He dined with Pharisees. Thus, "the Son of man came eating and drinking." Indeed, so free was His conduct in this respect, that sour and narrow-souled critics were able to call Him a gluttonous man and a wine-bibber. False as these nicknames were, they derived a colour of truth from His way of living; none would ever have dreamed of applying them to the Baptist.

This contrast is remarkable between two so closely associated as John and Jesus. Both were religious teachers, whose disciples imitated them; but in this particular their examples led in opposite directions. The disciples of John fasted, while Christ's disciples feasted. Could these opposite courses both be justified?

The Baptist no doubt had reasons for his conduct which satisfied himself. There are dangers in society. The lust of the flesh and the lust of the eyes and the pride of life are there. Company is the ruin of many a man and of many a family. There are social circles in which religion would not be tolerated, and there are others in which those who profess it are under sore temptation to hide their colours. The Baptist felt that these influences were so predominant in the society of his day that neither he nor his followers could bear up against them. The only alternatives between which they had to choose were either, on the one hand, to flee from society and keep their religion pure and entire or, on the other, to enter it and lose their religion; and there could be no doubt which was the path of duty.* Jesus, on the contrary, could

---

* John was well aware, however, of the imperfection of his own standpoint. "He pointed across to the sweetness, freedom and glory of the new dispensation, as Moses from Pisgah saw the land of promise."—SCHLEIERMACHER, *Predigten*, vol. iv. In this volume there are four discourses which may be called a kind of sketch of what has been attempted in this book. They are entitled—

Christ as a Teacher.
Christ as a Miracle-Worker.
Christ in Social Life.
Christ among His disciples.

go into society not only without striking His colours, but for the purpose of displaying them. So completely was His religious character the whole of Him, and so powerful and victorious were His principles, that there was no fear of any company He might enter obscuring His testimony for God. And He lent His followers the same power: He filled them with an enthusiasm which wrought in them like new wine; they moved through the world with the free and glad bearing of wedding guests; and therefore wherever they went they gave the tone to society; their enthusiasm was so exuberant that it was far more likely to set others on fire than to be extinguished by worldly influences.

Here we seem to find the true answer to the perplexing questions often raised as to how far the people of God ought to venture into society and take part in its engagements. What is its effect on your religious life and profession? Does it silence your testimony? does it cool down your enthusiasm? does it secularise you and render you unfit for prayer? If so, then you must adopt the Baptist's line of conduct and keep away from it, or seek for company in which your principles will be safe. But there are those who can venture far into the world and yet everywhere be true to their Saviour; they are known as Christians wherever they appear, and people respect their position; they would not go anywhere if they knew that their mouths were to be stopped on the subjects lying nearest their hearts; the energy of Christ in them is so glowing and victorious a force that they mould the society in which they are, instead of being moulded by it. This may be a difficult attainment; but there can be no doubt that it is the attitude towards the world most worthy of Christ's followers and like to His own.

II.

It has been mentioned how often He is recorded to have been present at feasts. This part of His conduct was of a piece with all the rest; for nothing He ever did, however trivial it might seem to be, was unconnected with the grand mission upon which He had come to the world. This mission was to make known the love of Heaven and to awaken and foster love on earth. He lived to increase the love of man to God and the love of man to man; and nothing which could serve either of these ends was unimportant in His eyes.

He encouraged hospitality because it promotes one of these ends: it helps to break down the obstacles which separate men and to bind them together in the bonds of goodwill. When men meet one another, the misconceptions and misunderstandings which have caused estrangement dissolve in the light of better acquaintance. How often we come away from a first conversation with one against whom we have entertained a prejudice with the remark that he is not a bad fellow after all; and not unfrequently after a social rencontre we carry away an enthusiastic admiration for a character which we have previously considered proud, or formal, or shallow. Our dislikes and suspicions breed and grow great at a distance, but they die at the touch of actual acquaintance.

Jesus did not regard even the courtesies of life as beneath His notice and encouragement. These foster respect between man and man, causing us to think of one another as personalities, not as things to be neglected or trampled on. Once He was invited to dine at a house where the host neglected to show Him the ordinary Oriental courtesies. The man had no real regard for his Guest, but invited Him for a selfish purpose of his own. He wished to gratify his curiosity by examining at leisure one who was the talk of the country and to honour himself by having the distinguished man beneath his roof. But he felt it to be a condescension, and he showed this by omitting the courtesies which he bestowed on the guests of his own standing. Jesus felt the slight; and, before leaving the table, He exposed Simon's little and loveless heart, enumerating one by one,* in tones of scathing indig-

---

* "Notanda sunt antitheta in quibus Simoni mulier præfertur: nempe quod hæc lachrymis suis rigavit Christi pedes, et capillis abstersit, quum ille ne vulgarem quidem aquam dari jussisset: quod hæc non desierit osculari pedes,

nation, the courtesies he had grudged Him. He could not enjoy a loveless feast.

Where, on the contrary, love was, He would not have it controlled. When, at the feast of another Simon, His gentle disciple Mary poured her costly treasure on His head and brought down on herself the reproaches of narrow hearts that grudged the extravagance, Jesus defended her against the pretended champions of the poor and insisted on love having its way.

It is a violation of the sacrament of hospitality when any other motive underlies it but love. Jesus pointed the finger of condemnation at those who extend hospitality only to guests who, they hope, will extend it to them in turn, thus degrading it to a business transaction. It is, if possible, a meaner motive still to make it only an opportunity of selfish display. Cumbrous luxury is the death of true hospitality. It narrows the scope of it; for even the wealthy can indulge but seldom in such extravagance, and people of humbler means are not able to face it at all except at the risk of ruin. This is one of the growing evils of the present day. With the money spent on a single tiresome feast, half a dozen simple and frugal entertainments might be furnished forth, and thus the scope of hospitality widened.* Instead of gorging the wealthy, who have too much already, influential entertainers might occasionally open their doors to those younger and humbler than themselves, and parents might assemble often round their tables

---

quum ille ne hospitali quidem osculo dignatus esset Christum excipere: quod pretiosum unguentum illa effuderit in pedes, hic autem ne oleo quidem caput unxerit."—CALVIN, *in loc*.

* "Hospitality is threefold:—for one's family, this is of necessity; for strangers, this is courtesy; for the poor, this is charity.

"To keep a disorderly house is the way to keep neither house nor lands. For whilst they keep the greatest roaring, their state steals away in the greatest silence. Yet, when many consume themselves with secret vices, then hospitality bears the blame; whereas it is not the meat but the sauce, not the supper but the gaming after it, doth undo them.

"Measure not the entertainment of a guest by HIS estate, but THINE OWN. Because he is a lord forget not that thou art but a gentleman; otherwise, if with feasting him thou breakest thyself, he will not cure thy rupture, and (perchance) may rather deride than pity thee."—FULLER, *The Holy and Profane State*.

suitable company for their children, instead of driving them to public places to seek occupation for their hours of leisure. There is a mission of social kindness still remaining to be opened up as one of the agencies of Christianity.

III.

Though the encouragement of hospitality, and through it of love, was one reason for which Jesus went to the tables of those who invited Him, He carried there a still higher purpose. When He went to dine at the house of Zacchæus, He said, "To-day is salvation come to this house;" and salvation came to many a house when He entered it. Hospitality affords unrivalled opportunities of conversation, and Jesus made use of these to speak words of eternal life. If you carefully examine His words, you will be surprised to find how many of them are literally table-talk— words spoken to His fellow-guests at meals. Some of His most priceless sayings, which are now the watchwords of His religion, were uttered in these commonplace circumstances, such as, "They that are whole have no need of a physician, but they that are sick;" "The Son of man is come to seek and to save that which was lost;" and many more.

This is an instance of how Jesus dignified life and found golden opportunities of doing good in those elements of it which are often treated as mere waste. The talk and the hilarity of the table are a snare. Men of social charm often use their gift to their own undoing and to the injury of others. The meeting-place of boon companions is to many the vestibule of ruin. Even where sociality is not permitted to degenerate into temptation, the conversation of the table is too often allowed to lapse into triviality and stupidity; and the meetings of friends, which might give intellectual stimulus and kindle noble purpose, become a weariness and satisfy nobody. It is a rare gift to be able to lift conversation out of the ditch and lead it to manly and profitable themes.

There have, however, been servants of God who in this respect have followed very closely in the footsteps of their Master.

They have made conversation a delightful and profitable art; and to enjoy their company in the free interchange of social intercourse has been an education in everything good and true. A man of note recently deceased, son of a father still more notable, has left a striking picture of the circle of scholars and men of God who used to be assembled round his father's hospitable table, and of the wonder and delight with which he and his brothers, then only children, used to listen to the discussions and pick up the crumbs of wisdom.* No parent can do his children a better service than by making his house a resort of the wise and good, in whom the keen observation of childhood may see examples of noble manhood and womanhood. "Be not forgetful," says the Epistle to the Hebrews, "to entertain strangers, for thereby some have entertained angels unawares;" on which one of the wise has thus commented: "By exercising hospitality—by treating with sympathy and hearty interest those who are still in many respects strangers to us—by showing ourselves kindly and opening our houses to them, as circumstances permit and opportunities offer—it may also happen to us to entertain angels; that is, men in whom we must recognise messengers sent to us from God, or from the world of mind and ideas, and whose sojourn in our house, whose conversation, whose influence on our souls, may bring us a blessing far outweighing all we can do for them."†

IV.

We have been looking at our Lord as the guest of others; but He comes before us in the Gospels also as Himself an entertainer.

---

* "Here almost every night, for long years, came Professors Dod and Maclean, and frequently Professors J. W. Alexander, Joseph Henry, and the older professors, A. Alexander, and Samuel Miller, President Carnahan, and frequently, when visiting the town, Professors Vethake and Torrey, and Dr. John W. Yeomans. Thus, at least in the eyes of the young sons gleaming out from the corners, from the shadows of which they looked on with breathless interest, this study became the scene of the most wonderful debates and discourses on the highest themes of philosophy, science, literature, theology, morals, and politics." —Rev. Dr. A. A. Hodge in *Princetoniana*, by Rev. C. A Salmond, M.A.

† MARTENSEN, *Christian Ethics*, vol. iii.

Jesus never, indeed, had a house of His own to which He could invite people. But on the two occasions when He fed the five thousand and the four thousand He acted as entertainer on a colossal scale.

It was a character in which He was thoroughly Himself; for it displayed His consideration for the common wants of man. Spiritual as He was and intent on the salvation of the soul, He never undervalued or overlooked the body. On the contrary, He recognised on it the stamp and honour of its Maker, and He knew quite well that it is often only through the body that the soul can be reached. The great majority of His guests were doubtless poor, and it gratified His generous heart to confer a benefit on them. It was, indeed, but common fare He gave them;* the table was the ground, the tablecloth was the green grass, and the banqueting hall was the open air; but never did His guests enjoy a better meal, for love presided at the table, and it is love that makes an entertainment fine.

As we see Him there, beaming with genial delight over the vast company, it is impossible not to think of such words of His as these: "I am the bread of life;" "The bread which I shall give is My flesh, which I will give for the life of the world." In His teaching He delighted to represent the gospel as a feast, to which He invited all the sons of men in the beautiful spirit of a royal host.

But nothing else shows so strikingly how characteristic of Him this spirit was as the fact that the memorial by which He has chosen to be remembered to all generations is a feast. He might have selected any one of a hundred other mementoes. He might, for instance, have instituted among His followers a periodical fast. But this would have been a thoroughly unsuitable memorial of Him; for His is a gospel of abundance, joy and union. He chose what was fitting and truly significant; and so throughout all ages at the head of His own table the Saviour sits in the character of Entertainer, His face radiant with goodwill and His heart over-

---

* "Barley loaves," the bread of the poor.

flowing with generosity; and over His head, on the wall behind where He sits, these words are written, "This Man receiveth sinners, and eateth with them."

VII.

Christ as a Man of Prayer

Matt.	xi. 25, 26.
	xiv. 19.
	xix. 13.
	xxi. 12, 13.
	xxvi. 53.
Luke	ix. 18.
	xi. 1.
John	vi. 23.
	xiv. 16, 17.
	xvii.
Matt.	xiv. 23.
Mark	i. 35.
	xiv. 22, 23.
Luke	v. 16.
Matt.	xxvi. 36-44.
Luke	vi. 12, 13.
Luke	iii. 21, 22.
	ix. 28, 29.
John	xi. 41, 42.

CHAPTER VII.

Christ as a Man of Prayer.

I.

There is surely a mystery in the prayers of Jesus. If, as we believe, He was no less than God, how could God pray to God, or what need could there be in His nature for the satisfaction of which He required to pray?

It may be a partial answer to this question to say that all prayer does not consist of petitions arising from the sense of need. Prayer, indeed, is often spoken of, especially by those who wish to bring it into ridicule, as if it consisted of nothing but a series of demands addressed to God—to give fine weather, or to take away disease, or in some other way to alter our circumstances in accordance with our wishes. But it is not by those who pray that prayer is thus spoken of. In the prayers of those who pray most and best, petitions proper, I venture to say, occupy only an inconsiderable place. Much of prayer expresses the fulness of the soul rather than its emptiness. It is the overflow of the cup. Prayer at its best is, if one may be allowed the expression, conversation with God, the confidential talk of a child who tells everything to his father. There is a remarkable example of this in the *Confessions* of St. Augustine. This great book is in the form of a prayer from beginning to end; yet it narrates its author's history and expounds the most important of his opinions. Evidently the good man had got into the habit of doing all his deepest thinking in the form of conversation with God.

If this be what prayer is, it is not difficult to understand how the Eternal Son should have prayed to the Eternal Father. Indeed, it is easy to see that, in this sense, He must have prayed without ceasing.

But this does not altogether clear up the mystery of the prayers of Jesus; for many of them were undoubtedly expressions of the sense of want. "In the days of His flesh, He offered up prayers and supplications with strong crying and tears unto Him that was able to save Him from death, and was heard in that He feared."* How can we explain a statement like this? There is but one explanation of it; and it is His true humanity. It is only by accepting this truth in the fullest sense that we can understand this aspect of His life. Christ was not half a God and half a man, but perfectly God and perfectly man. There are things about Him, and there are statements of His own, to which justice cannot be done without categorically calling Him God. We may hesitate to utter this confession, but the facts, unless we flinch from them, will compel us to make it. On the other hand, there are other things about Him which compel us in the fullest acceptation of the term to call Him a man; and we are not honouring but dishonouring Him if we do not accept this truth also in all its fulness and in all its consequences.

He prayed, then, because He was a man. Humanity even at its best is a feeble and dependent thing; it can never be self-sufficient. Even in Him it was not sufficient for itself, but dependent on God from day to day; and He expressed His sense of dependence by praying. Does this not bring Him very near us? Verily He is our brother, bone of our bone and flesh of our flesh.

But there is another lesson in it, and a graver one. Although a man, Jesus was a sinless man. At every stage of development His manhood was perfect. He had no sinful past to weaken the

* Heb. v. 7.

force of present effort. Yet He needed prayer and resorted to it continually. What a commentary on our need of it! If He needed it, being what He was, how must we need it, being what we are.

II.

The life of prayer is a secret life, and everyone who really loves prayer has habits of it known only to himself. Much of the prayerfulness of Jesus must have lain beyond the observation of even His disciples, and therefore is altogether unrecorded in the Gospels. But some of His habits have been preserved, and they are extremely interesting and instructive.

He liked, when about to pray, to escape from the house and from the town and go away out into the natural solitudes. We read, "He went out and departed unto a solitary place, and there prayed." Elsewhere it is said, "He withdrew Himself into the wilderness, and prayed." He seems to have especially loved mountains as places of prayer. When the statement is anywhere made that He went up to a mountain to pray, commentators try to find out, by examining the vicinity in which He was sojourning at the time, which mountain it was He ascended for this purpose. But in this, I think, they are on the wrong track. In Palestine, as in many parts of Scotland, there is mountain everywhere. A mile or two from any town you are out on it. You have only to quit the houses, cross a few acres of cultivated ground, and your feet are on the turfy pastures, where you can be absolutely alone. Jesus had, if we may so speak, made the discovery that He could obtain this solitude anywhere; and, when He arrived in a town, His first thought was, which was the shortest road to the mountain,—just as ordinary travellers inquire where are the most noted sights and which is the best hotel.

There is a solitude of time as well as a solitude of space. What mountains and wildernesses are to towns and cities, the night-time and the early morning are to the day-time and the early night. Jesus frequented this solitude too for prayer. We hear of Him continuing the whole night in prayer to God; or it is said that

He "rose up a great while before day, and departed into a solitary place to pray."

It may partly have been because, on account of His poverty, He could not easily find solitude in the houses in which He lodged that Jesus cultivated this habit,* and this may give His example a special interest for any whose circumstances expose them to the same difficulty. But it is a discovery which might immensely enrich us all if we were to realise how easy it is to get into the natural solitudes. There is scarcely a town out of which you cannot escape in a very few minutes and find yourself quite alone—on a bit of shore, or on a mountain, or in a pasture or a wood. The town or city may be thundering away quite near, with its imprisoned multitudes bound on the treadmill of its toils or its amusements; but you are out of it and alone with God.

There is more than mere solitude in such a situation to assist prayer. There is a ministry of nature which soothes the mind and disposes it to devotion. Never did I feel more strongly that in this habit Jesus had laid bare one of the great secrets of life than one day when I climbed all alone a hill above Inveraray and lay on the summit of it, musing through a summer forenoon. On every hand there stretched a solitary world of mountain and moorland; the loch below was gleaming in the sun like a shield of silver; the town was visible at the foot of the hill, and the passengers could be seen moving in the streets, but no sound of its bustle reached

---

* Many of us may be able to be quite alone in our own homes. Jesus recognised this when He said: "Enter thou, when thou prayest, into thy closet; and, when thou hast shut thy door, pray to thy Father which is in secret." The essential thing is to have the world shut out and to be alone with God. It is for this reason that we shut our eyes in prayer: it is that our attention, being withdrawn from all sights and sounds without, may be concentrated on the vision and the voices within. We may even so familiarise ourselves with the inward world that we shall acquire the habit of transporting ourselves into it at will at any hour of the day and in any circumstances. Amidst the whirr of machinery, in the bustle of the street, even in the midst of conversation, we may be able mentally to disappear out of time and stand for an instant in eternity face to face with God; and few prayers are more precious than the momentary ejaculations offered in the course of daily occupations. He who has acquired this habit has a strong tower into which he can retreat in every time of need.

so high. The great sky was over all; and God seemed just at hand, waiting to hear every word. It was in spots like this that Jesus prayed.

He prayed, however, in company as well as in solitude. We hear of Him again and again taking two or three of His disciples away to pray with them, and sometimes of Him praying with them all. The Twelve were a kind of family to Him, and He assiduously cultivated family worship. He spoke too of the value of united prayer. "I say unto you, that if two of you shall agree on earth as touching anything that they shall ask, it shall be done for them of My Father which is in heaven." United prayer acts on the spirit very much in the same way as conversation acts on the mind. Many a man's intellect, when he is alone, is slow in its movements and far from fertile in the production of ideas. But, when it meets with another mind and clashes with it in conversation, it is transformed: it becomes agile and audacious, it burns and coruscates, and brings forth ideas out of its resources which are a surprise even to itself.* So, where two or three are met together, the prayer of one strikes fire from the soul of another; and the latter in his turn leads the way to nobler heights of devotion. And lo! as their joy increases, there is One in their midst whom they all recognise and cling to. He was there before, but it is only when their hearts begin to burn that they recognise Him; and in a true sense they may be said to bring Him there—"Where two or three are met together in My name, there am I in the midst of them."

III.

The occasions which call for prayer are innumerable, and it would be vain to attempt to count them. Jesus undoubtedly had,

---

* "Certain it is, that whosoever hath his Mind fraught with many Thoughts, his Wits and Understanding do clarify and break up, in the communicating and discoursing with Another: he tosseth his Thoughts more easily; he marshalleth them more orderly; he seeth how they look when they are turned into Words; finally, he waxeth wiser than himself, and that more by an Hour's Discourse than by a Day's Meditation."—*Bacon's Essays*, xxvii: Of Friendship.

as we have ourselves, new reasons for praying every day; but some of the occasions on which He prayed are specially instructive.

1. We find Him engaged in special prayer just before taking very important steps in life. One of the most important steps He ever took was the selection from among His disciples of the Twelve who were to be His apostles. It was an act on which the whole future of Christianity depended; and what was He doing before it took place? "It came to pass in those days that He went into a mountain to pray, and continued all night in prayer to God; and, when it was day, He called unto Him His disciples, and of them He chose twelve, whom He also named apostles." It was after this night-long vigil that He proceeded to the choice which was to be so momentous for Him and for them and for all the world. There was another day for which, we are told, He made similar preparation. It was that on which He first informed His disciples that He was to suffer and die.

Thus it is evident that, when Jesus had a day of crisis or of difficult duty before Him, He gave Himself specially to prayer. Would it not simplify our difficulties if we attacked them in the same way? It would infinitely increase the intellectual insight with which we try to penetrate a problem and the power of the hand we lay upon duty. The wheels of existence would move far more smoothly and our purposes travel more surely to their aims, if every morning we reviewed beforehand the duties of the day with God.*

---

* In Nicoll's *Life of Jesus Christ*, pp. 178-80, an important consideration is added: "Jesus Christ not only prayed before great and decisive acts, but He prayed after them. . . . This teaches us much which it is easy but fatal to miss. When we have done some great work by immense expenditure of force, we are tempted to say our part is done,—we cannot accomplish more. Many a man desires to end and crown his public life amidst the shoutings of applause for some victory or achievement. He would retire to boast of it, and live all the rest of his days upon that proud memory. Better it is to pray,—to pray, if it be God's will, fix new strength, for new if humbler efforts, and, if that is denied, for blessing on what has been attempted or done. Jesus Christ did not boast, He did not give up, but He recruited Himself for new service by continuing in prayer to

2. Jesus appears to have devoted Himself specially to prayer at times when His life was unusually full of work and excitement. His was a very busy life; there were nearly always "many coming and going" about Him. Sometimes, however, there was such a congestion of thronging objects that He had scarcely time to eat. But even then He found time to pray. Indeed, these appear to have been with Him seasons of more prolonged prayer than usual. Thus we read: "So much the more went there a fame abroad of Him, and great multitudes came together to hear and to be healed by Him of their infirmities; but He withdrew Himself into the wilderness and prayed."

Many in our day know what this congestion of occupations is: they are swept off their feet with their engagements and can scarcely find time to eat. We make this a reason for not praying; Jesus made it a reason for praying. Is there any doubt which is the better course ? Many of the wisest have in this respect done as Jesus did. When Luther had a specially busy and exciting day, he allowed himself longer time than usual for prayer beforehand. A wise man once said that he was too busy to be in a hurry; he meant that, if he allowed himself to become hurried, he could not do all that he had to do. There is nothing like prayer for producing this calm self-possession. When the dust of business so fills

---

God. Another temptation is to pride. We are lifted above the simplicity and humility in which we lived before. Our hearts swell, and we are tempted to think our previous life mean and insignificant. Never are we further from God than when intoxicated by pride. In the pride of their hearts the wicked angels fell, and we may fall too unless we are delivered from their sin. Nothing will avail more effectually to allay and silence our pride than prayer. In communion with our Father our pride is chilled and destroyed. A kindred temptation after great achievements is the temptation to profound depression. When one has done one's utmost, and put forth the whole force of life, one feels completely spent, as if work were over. Men who have preached with power to multitudes of people have told us of the terrible languor which succeeds a full outburst of the heart. They have told us how they felt as if their life went from them in that supreme effort, and could never be regained. That is natural; and we may learn from Jesus Christ how it is to be met. Let us pray that by prayer and service we may be taught to feel that our well-springs are in God, and that He who strengthened and filled us for that achievement, which we fear we can never repeat, can gird us, if He will, for new and nobler work."

your room that it threatens to choke you, sprinkle it with the water of prayer, and then you can cleanse it out with comfort and expedition.

3. We find Jesus engaging in special prayer when about to enter into temptation. The greatest scene of prayer in His life is undoubtedly Gethsemane. As we enter that garden after Him, we fear almost to look on the scene—it is so sacred and so passes our understanding; and we tremble as we listen to the prayers rising from the ground where He lies. Never were prayers heard like these. We cannot fathom them; yet much may be learned from them. Let one lesson, however, suffice in the meantime: He prayed on this occasion before entering into temptation; for at the gate of the garden, after the agony was over, He said, "This is your hour and the power of darkness." It was the commencement of His final conflict with the powers of wickedness in earth and hell. But He had equipped Himself for the conflict by the prayer in the garden beforehand, and so He was able to go through all that followed with unruffled dignity and with perfect success. His strength was the strength of prayer.

What an illustration of contrast was presented on that occasion by the weakness of the disciples! For them also the hour and the power of darkness began at the gate of Gethsemane; but it was an hour of disaster and ignominious defeat. Why? Because they were sleeping when they ought to have been praying. "Watch and pray," He had said, bending over their prostrate forms, "lest ye enter into temptation." But they heeded not; and so, when the hour of temptation came, they fell. Alas! their experience has often been ours also. The only armour in which temptation can be successfully met is prayer; and, when the enemy is allowed to come upon us before we have buckled it on, we have not a chance of standing.

4. If any scene of prayer in our Lord's life may compete in interest with this one, it is the last of all. Jesus died praying. His last words were words of prayer. The habit of life was strong in death. It may seem far off; but this event will come to us also.

What will our last words be? Who can tell? But would it not be beautiful if our spirit were so steeped in the habit of prayer that the language of prayer came naturally to us at the last? Many have died with Christ's own last words on their lips. Who would not covet them for his own? "Father, into Thy hands I commend My spirit."

IV.

If anyone were to go through the life of Christ seeking for answers to His prayers, many of them, I am persuaded, could be found. But I shall at present refer only to two on which the Word itself lays emphasis, and which are specially instructive.

The Transfiguration was an answer to prayer. This is how it is introduced in one of the Gospels: "And it came to pass about an eight days after these sayings, He took Peter and John and James, and went up into a mountain to pray. And as He prayed, the fashion of His countenance was altered, and His raiment was white and glistering. And, behold, there talked with Him two men, which were Moses and Elias." I do not say that He was praying for this alteration in His countenance and raiment, or even for the privilege of talking with these wise and sympathetic spirits about the work which He was about to accomplish at Jerusalem. But yet, I say, all this was in answer to the prayer He was offering when it came. There are some who, disbelieving in the direct virtue of prayer to obtain from God what it asks, yet believe in what they call the reflex influence of prayer: they allow it does you good to pray, even if you get nothing directly by it, and even if there is no God to hear you. This, taken as the whole theory of prayer, is a mockery, as the simplest mind must perceive. But it is none the less true that there is a most blessed reflex influence of prayer. Prayers for goodness and purity in a sense answer themselves; for you cannot pray for these things without in some measure receiving them in the very act. To lift up the soul to God calms and ennobles it. It was this, I imagine, that was the beginning of Christ's transfiguration. The absorption and delight of communion with His Father overspread His very face with beauty and glory; and through this outlet the inner glory leapt forth. In some degree this happens to all who pray, and it may happen in a high degree to those who pray much. Moses, after being forty days in the mount with God, shone with the same kind of light as the disciples saw in their Master on the Holy Mount; and there is a spiritual beauty bestowed in some degree on all God's saints who pray much which is of the same nature and is the most precious of all answers to prayer. Character flows from the well-spring of prayer.

The other answer to prayer given to Jesus to which I desire to call attention took place at His baptism. Here is St. Luke's account of it: "Now when all the people were baptized, it came to pass, that Jesus also being baptized, and praying, the heaven was opened, and the Holy Ghost descended like a dove upon Him." It was when He was praying that the Spirit was sent down upon Him, and in all probability it was this which at the moment He was praying for. He had just left His home in Nazareth to begin His public work; and He was in immediate need of the Holy Spirit to equip Him for His task. It is a forgotten truth that Jesus was filled with the Holy Ghost; but it is one most clearly revealed in the Gospels. The human nature of Jesus was from first to last dependent on the Holy Ghost, being thereby made a fit organ for the divine; and it was in the strength of this inspiration that all His work, as preacher, miracle-worker and atoner, was done.* And if

---

* "The Holy Spirit, in a peculiar manner, anointed Him with all those *extraordinary powers and gifts* which were necessary for the exercise and discharging of His office on the earth. Isa. lxi 1: 'The Spirit of the Lord God is upon Me; because the Lord hath anointed Me to preach good tidings unto the meek: He hath sent Me to bind up the broken-hearted, to proclaim liberty to the captives, and the opening of the prison to them that are bound.' It is the prophetical office of Christ, and His discharge thereof in His ministry on the earth, which is intended. And He applies these words unto Himself with respect unto His preaching of the Gospel (Luke iv. 18, 19); for this was that office which He principally attended unto here in the world, as that whereby He instructed men in the nature and use of His other offices. . . . Hereunto was He fitted by this unction

in any measure our life is to be an imitation of His—if we are to help in carrying on His work in the world or in filling up what is lacking in His sufferings—we must be dependent on the same influence. But how are we to get it? He has told us Himself: "If ye then, being evil, know how to give good gifts unto your children, how much more shall your heavenly Father give the Holy Spirit to them that ask Him." Power, like character, comes from the fountain of prayer.

---

of the Spirit. And here, also, is a distinction between the 'Spirit that was upon Him,' and His being 'anointed to preach,' which contains the communication of the gifts of that Spirit unto Him. . . . And this collation of extraordinary gifts for the discharge of His prophetical office was at His baptism (Matt. iii. 17). They were not bestowed on the Head of the Church, nor are any gifts of the same nature in general bestowed on any of His members, but for use, exercise, and improvement. And that they were then collated appears; for,—

"1. Then did He receive the *visible pledge* which confirmed Him in, and testified unto others His calling of God to, the exercise of His *office*; for then 'the Spirit of God descended like a dove, and lighted upon Him: and, lo, a voice came from heaven, saying, This is My beloved Son, in whom I am well pleased' (Matt. iii. 16,17). Hereby was He 'sealed of God the Father' (John vi. 27) in that visible pledge of His vocation, setting the great seal of heaven to His commission. And this also was to be a testimony unto others, that they might own Him in His office, now He had undertaken to discharge it (chap. i. 33).

"2. He now entered on His public ministry, and wholly *gave Himself up* unto His work; for before He did only occasionally manifest the presence of God with Him, somewhat to prepare the minds of men to attend unto His ministry, as when He filled them with astonishment at His discourses with the doctors in the Temple (Luke ii. 46, 47). And although it is probable that He might be acted by the Spirit in and unto many such extraordinary actions during His course of a private life, yet the fulness of gifts for His work He received not until the time of His baptism, and therefore before that He gave not Himself up wholly unto His public ministry.

"3. Immediately hereon it is said that *He was 'full of the Holy Ghost'* (Luke iv. 1). Before, He was said to 'wax strong in spirit,' πληρούμενος σοφίας, chap. ii. 40, 'continually filling'; but now He is πλήρης Πνεύματος Ἁγίου ('full of the Holy Ghost'). He was actually possessed of and furnished with all that fulness of spiritual gifts which were any way needful for Him or useful unto Him, or which human nature is capable of receiving."

OWEN, *On the Holy Spirit*

VIII.

Christ as a Student of Scripture

Matt.	iv. 4, 7, 10.
	v. 17, 48.
	vi. 29.
	vii. 12.
	viii. 4, 11.
	ix. 13.
	x. 15.
	xi. 21, 24.
	xii. 3-7, 39-42.
	xiii. 14, 15.
	xv. 7-9.
	xix. 8, 18, 19.
	xxi. 16, 42.
	xxii. 29-32, 35-40, 43-45.
	xxiv. 37-39.
	xxvi. 30, 31, 53, 54.
	xxvii. 46.
Luke	iv. 16-27.
	viii. 21.
	xvi. 29, 30.
	xxiii. 46.
	xxiv. 27.
John	v. 39, 45, 46.
	vi. 32, 45, 49.
	vii. 19, 22.
	viii. 17, 37.
	x. 34, 35.
	xiii. 18.
	xvii. 12, 14, 17.

CHAPTER VIII.

Christ as a Student of Scripture.

I.

It is probable that Jesus knew three languages. The language of His country was Aramaic; and some fragments of it, as they fell from His lips, have been preserved to us in the Gospels, such as *Talitha, cumi,* the words with which He raised the daughter of Jairus. But it is not likely that He read the Scriptures in this His native tongue. Sometimes, indeed, the quotations of the Old Testament in the New do not tally exactly with any form of the Old Testament now in our hands, and the conjecture has been hazarded that in such cases the quotations are taken from an Aramaic version then in existence; but this is no more than conjecture.

Another language He spoke was Greek. In Galilee, where He was brought up, there were so many Greek settlers that it was called "Galilee of the Gentiles;" and Greek was the language of commerce and of the more cosmopolitan kind of social intercourse. A boy brought up in Galilee in those days would have the same chance of learning Greek as in our day a boy brought up in the Highlands of Scotland has of learning English. Now in Greek there existed in Christ's time a version of the Old Testament Scriptures. We still possess it, under the name of the Septuagint, or Seventy, the supposed number of the translators who executed it in Egypt between two and three hundred years before the Christian era. It was extensively circulated in Palestine. The New Testament writers very frequently quote from it, and there is little doubt that our Lord read it.

The third language which He probably knew was Hebrew. This can only be stated as a probability; for, though Hebrew was the language of the Jews, it had ceased before Christ's time to be the spoken language of Palestine. Languages sometimes decay even in the countries to which they are native, and become so mixed with foreign elements as to lose their identity. A modern example is seen in Italy, where Latin is now a dead language, having been transmuted by slow degrees in the course of centuries into Italian. Though Italian bears considerable resemblance to the ancient tongue, the boys of Italy of to-day have to learn Latin just as our own boys do. The same thing had taken place in Palestine. The Hebrew language, in which the Old Testament was written, had degenerated into Aramaic; and Jews who desired to read the Scriptures in the original tongue had to learn the dead language. There is reason to believe that Jesus acquired it. In some of His quotations from the Old Testament, scholars have observed, He purposely diverges from the Greek and reverts to the exact terms of the original. It will be remembered also that in the synagogue of Nazareth He was asked to read the Scriptures. Now it is probable that in the synagogue-roll the writing was in Hebrew, the reader having first to read it in that language and then to translate it into the language of the people.* If this be so, it is surely interesting to think of Jesus learning the dead language in order to read the Word of God in the tongue in which it was written. Remember, His condition in life was only that of a mechanic; and it may have been in the brief intervals of toil that He mastered the strange letters and forms that were to bring Him face to face with

---

* "Vers für Vers, abwechselnd mit dem dazu bestellten Uebersetzer, las der Aufgerufene den Text und der Uebersetzer sprach das Targum, d. h. die aramäische Paraphrase."—HAUSRATH, *Neutestamentliche Zeitgeschichte.*

the Psalms as David wrote them and with the prophecies as they flowed from the pen of Isaiah or Jeremiah. In our own country the same sacred ambition is not unknown. At all events, a generation ago there were working men who learned Greek with the grammar stuck on the loom in front of them, that they might read the New Testament in the language in which it was written; and I have spoken with the members of a group of business men in Edinburgh who met every Saturday to read the Greek Testament. Certainly there is a flavour about the Bible, when read in the language it was written in, which it loses more or less in every translation; and it is perhaps surprising that in our day, when the love of the Bible is so common and the means of learning are so accessible, the ambition to read it thus is not more widely spread.

It is pathetic to think that Jesus never possessed a Bible of His own; but there can be no doubt of the fact. The expense of such a possession in those days was utterly beyond the means of one in His condition; and besides, the bulkiness of the rolls on which it was written would have prevented it from being portable, even if He could have possessed it. Possibly in His home there may have been a few of the precious rolls, containing the Psalms or other favourite portions of Holy Writ; but it must have been by frequenting the synagogue and obtaining access to the books lying there, perhaps through ingratiating Himself with their keeper, as an enthusiastic musician may do with the organist of a church in order to be permitted to use the instrument, that He was able to quench His thirst for sacred knowledge. We can procure the Holy Book for next to nothing, and every child possesses a copy. May its cheapness and universal currency never make it in our eyes a common thing!

Of course it was only the Old Testament Jesus had to read. It may be worth while to recall this as a reminder of how much more reason we have to love and prize our larger Bible. When I read in the Psalms such outbursts of affection for the Word of God as these: "Oh how I love Thy law: it is my study all the day;" "How sweet are Thy words to my taste; yea, sweeter than honey to my mouth;" "More to be desired are they than gold, yea, than much fine gold; sweeter also than honey and the honeycomb,"— I say, when I read such outbursts of holy feeling, and recollect that they came from the lips of men who possessed only the Old Testament, perhaps only a fragment of it—men in whose Bible there were no Gospels, or Epistles of Paul, or Apocalypse, who had never read the Sermon on the Mount or the Prodigal Son, the seventeenth of John or the eighth of Romans, the thirteenth of First Corinthians or the eleventh of Hebrews,—I ask what my feelings are towards the much larger Bible I possess, and I say to myself that surely in modern times the heart of man has become ossified, and the fountains of gratitude have dried up, and the fires of admiration and enthusiasm have been put out, so tame, in comparison, is our affection for the far more perfect Book.*

II.

There is the most indubitable evidence that Jesus was an assiduous student of the Word of God. This is furnished, not by repeated statements to this effect, but by proofs far more impressive. His recorded sayings abound with quotations from it. These are sometimes express references to the book and the verse; but

---

* No nobler tribute has been ever paid to the Divine Word than Edward Irving's *Orations for the Oracles of God*. We quote a few sentences from the first of them: "There is no express stirring up of faculties to meditate her high and heavenly strains—nor formal sequestration of the mind from all other concerns on purpose for her special entertainment—nor pause of solemn seeking and solemn waiting for a spiritual frame, before entering and listening to the voice of the Almighty's wisdom. Who feels the sublime dignity there is in a saying fresh descended from the porch of heaven? Who feels the awful weight there is in the least iota that hath dropped from the lips of God? Who feels the thrilling fear or trembling hope there is in words whereon the eternal destinies of himself do hang? Who feels the tide of gratitude swelling within his breast, for redemption and salvation, instead of flat despair and everlasting retribution? Or who, in perusing the Word of God, is captivated through all his faculties, transported through all his emotions, and through all his energies of action wound up? . . .

"Oh! if books had but tongues to speak their wrongs, then might this book well exclaim—Hear, O heavens! and give ear, O earth! I came from the love and embrace of God, and mute nature, to whom I brought no boon, did me rightful

oftener they are allusions to Old Testament events and person-ages or unexpressed quotations so woven into the warp and woof of His own statements as to show that the Old Testament drenched His mind through and through, supplied the scenery in which His imagination habitually worked, and moulded the very language in which He thought and spoke.

If His quotations are examined, it will be found that they are derived from every part of the book, showing His acquaintance not only with its prominent features, but with its obscurest cor-ners; so that we ourselves need not travel anywhere among the Old Testament writings without the assurance that His blessed feet have been there before us. It is, however, peculiarly enjoy-able in the reading of Scripture to be able to halt at a text and know for certain, from His quoting it, that out of this very vessel, which we are raising to our lips, Jesus drank the living water. There are even texts which we may without irreverence call His favourites, because He quoted them again and again. And there are books of Scripture which seem to have been specially dear to Him, Deuteronomy, the Psalms, and Isaiah being the chief.

Not long ago it fell to my lot to look over the papers of a deceased friend. As all who have had the same duty to perform

---

homage. To man I came, and my words were to the children of men. I disclosed to you the mysteries of the hereafter, and the secrets of the throne of God. I set open to you the gates of salvation, and the way of eternal life, heretofore unknown. Nothing in heaven did I withhold from your hope and ambition; and upon your earthly lot I poured the full horn of divine providence and consola-tion. But ye requited me with no welcome, ye held no festivity on my arrival: ye sequester me from happiness and heroism, closeting me with sickness and infir-mity; ye make not of me, nor use me for your guide to wisdom and prudence, but press me into your list of duties, and withdraw me to a mere corner of your time; and most of ye set me at nought, and utterly disregard me. I came, the ful-ness of the knowledge of God: angels delighted in my company, and desired to dive into my secrets. But ye, mortals, place masters over me, subjecting me to the discipline and dogmatism of men, and tutoring me in your schools of learn-ing. I came not to be silent in your dwellings, but to speak welfare to you and to your children. I came to rule, and my throne to set up in the hearts of men. Mine ancient residence was the bosom of God; no residence will I have but the soul of an immortal; and if you had entertained me, I should have possessed you of the peace which I had with God."

must know, it is a pathetic task. There is a haunting sense of dese-cration in rifling the secrets kept hidden during life and learning exactly what the man was beneath the surface. My friend had been a man of the world, exposed to many of the temptations of those who have to do its business and mingle with its company; but he had sustained the character of a religious man. I had now the means of finding out whether this was something put on from the outside or growing from within. It was with deep awe that, as I advanced, I came upon evidence after evidence of an inner life with even deeper and fresher roots than I had ventured to hope for. When I opened his Bible especially, it told an unmistakable story; for the marks of long and diligent use were visible on every page—the leaves well worn, the choice texts underlined, short breathings of the heart noted on the margins. In some parts the marks of use were peculiarly frequent. This was the case espe-cially with Psalms, Isaiah and Hosea in the Old Testament and the writings of St. John in the New. I now knew the reality of the life that was ended, and whence its virtues had sprung.

Thus the very aspect of a man's Bible may be a record of his most secret habits and remain to those who come after him a monument of his religion or irreligion. To the living man himself there is perhaps no better test of his own religious condition than a glance through its pages; for by the tokens of use or neglect he may learn whether or not he loves it. I copied from the flyleaf of my friend's Bible a few words which perhaps explain the source of true love to the Word: "Oh, to come nearer to Christ, nearer to God, nearer to holiness! Every day to live more completely in Him, by Him, for and with Him. There is a Christ; shall I be Christless? A cleansing; shall I remain foul? A Father's love; shall I be an alien? A heaven; shall I be cast out?"

III.

There are different methods of studying the Scriptures with profit. On these we have no express teaching from the lips of

Christ; but from the records of His conduct we can see that He practised them.

According to the method by which it is studied, God's Word serves different uses in spiritual experience; one method being serviceable for one kind of use, and another for another. Jesus displayed perfect proficiency in all the ways of using it; and from this we are able to infer how He studied it.

There are especially three prominent uses to which we find Him putting the Bible, and these are very important for our imitation.

1. *For Defence*

The very first use we find Him making of the Word is as a defence against temptation. When the Wicked One came to Him and tempted Him in the wilderness, He answered every suggestion with, "It is written." The Word was in His hands the sword of the Spirit, and He turned with its edge the onsets of the enemy.

In like manner He defended Himself with it against the assaults of wicked men. When they lay in wait for Him and tried to entangle Him in His talk, He foiled them with the Word of God. Especially on that great day of controversy immediately before His end,* when all His enemies set upon Him and the champions of the different parties did their utmost to confuse and confute Him, He repelled their attacks one after another with answers drawn from the Scriptures; and at last silenced them and put them to shame in the eyes of the people by showing their ignorance of the Scriptures of which they were the chosen interpreters.

There was yet another enemy He met with the same weapon. It was the last enemy. When the terrors of death were closing round Him, like a dark multitude pressing in upon a solitary man, He had recourse to His old and tried weapon. Two at least, if not more, of His seven last words from the cross were verses out of His favourite book of Psalms. One of them was His very last

---

* Matt. xxii.

word, and with it He plucked His soul out of the jaws of death: "Father, into Thy hands I commend My spirit."

For this use of Scripture the practice of committing it to memory is essential. In every case I have mentioned Jesus was able to recur to the contents of a memory stored with texts of Scripture and find at once the necessary weapon for the occasion. Often, when temptation comes, there is no time to search for the word to meet it; everything depends on being already armed, with sword in hand. This shows how necessary it is to fill the memory, while it is plastic, with stores of texts; we do not know what use we may get of them in future days of trial and weakness. In daily reading, when we have gone through a chapter, it is an excellent plan to select a single verse and commit it to memory. Not only does this sharpen the attention on the whole chapter, but it lays up ammunition for future battles.

2. *For Inspiration*

It is easy from Christ's Old Testament references to see that He dwelt much among the great spirits of the past whose lives the Old Testament records. His earthly environment was unsympathetic in the extreme. In His own home He was not believed in. In His own country there was living an evil generation, as He often said, irresponsive to every motive that most profoundly affected Him. His own followers were, in mind and spirit, but children, whom He was only training to comprehend His ideas. His overcharged heart longed for companionship, and He had to seek it among the great figures of the past. In the silent walks and groves of Scripture He met with Abraham and Moses, with David and Elijah and Isaiah, and many more of kindred spirit. These men had lived for aims similar to His own. They had suffered for them as He was suffering; He could borrow the very words of Isaiah about his contemporaries to describe His own. If Jerusalem was persecuting Him, she had always been the city that slew the prophets. So near did He get in His reading of the Word to these departed spirits, so alive in His meditations did they become, that at last two of them, the greatest of all, Moses and Elias, were actually drawn back across the boundary of visibility and appeared conversing with Him in the Holy Mount. But this conversation was only the culmination of hundreds He had held before with them and with the other prophets in the pages of Holy Writ.

To enjoy this use of the Bible a different kind of study of it is necessary from that which makes it useful for defence. For defence the verbal memory of single texts is what is necessary; for inspiration our study must take a wider sweep. It must embrace the life of a man from beginning to end; it must understand the time which produced him and the circumstances against which he had to react. We must read about the man till we see the world of his day, and him moving in it; we must learn to catch his tone and accent. Then he is ours; he will walk with us; he will speak to us; he will be our companion and friend. This is the privilege of the Christian who knows his Bible: whatever be his surroundings in the actual world, he can transport himself at will into the best of company, where the brow of every one is crowned with nobleness, every eye beams encouragement, and the air is redolent of faith and hope and love.

3. *For Guidance*

Jesus used His Bible as the chart of His own life. Learned men, ay, and reverent men, have discussed the question at what age He became fully aware that He was the Messiah, and by what degrees He became possessed of a distinct knowledge of the path which He was to pursue: at what point, for example, He learned that He was to be not a victorious but a suffering Saviour; and they have supposed that He came to the knowledge of these things by the study of the prophecies of the Old Testament about Himself. I have never felt myself fit for such speculations; these things seem to me to be hidden behind the curtain of the mystery of His person as God and man in one. But it is easy in His words to see that He did follow His own course with intense interest in Old Testament prophecy, as in a chart. Again and again it is said

He did this and that, that such and such a prophecy might be fulfilled. To the deputation sent from the Baptist, and to others, He pointed out how literally His way of life corresponded with the portrait of the Messiah sketched by Isaiah and other prophets. His intercourse with His disciples after His resurrection seems to have been mainly devoted to showing them from Moses and all the prophets that His life, sufferings and death were the exact fulfilment of all that had been foretold.

To use Scripture thus requires a method of study far more advanced than is necessary for the uses of defence or inspiration already explained: it requires the power of taking a bird's-eye view of Scripture as a whole, of discerning the main currents flowing through it from first to last, and especially of tracing clearly the great central current to which all the others tend and into which they finally empty themselves.

Evidently this was Christ's way of studying the Bible: He could lift it up and wield it as a whole. One sees this even in His mode of using single texts. He rarely quotes a text without revealing in it some hidden meaning which no one had suspected before, but which shines clearly to all eyes as soon as it has been pointed out.* Some rare men in all ages have had this power. You occasionally hear a preacher who can quote a text so that it becomes transfigured and shines in his argument like a gem. What gives this power? It comes when the mind can go down and down through the text till it reaches the great lake of light that lies

---

* "Lord, this morning I read a chapter in the Bible, and therein observed a memorable passage, whereof I never took notice before. Why now, and no sooner, did I see it? Formerly my eyes were as open, and the letters as legible. Is there not a thin veil laid over Thy Word, which is more rarefied by reading, and at last wholly worn away? . . . I see the oil of Thy word will never leave increasing whilst any bring an empty barrel. The Old Testament will still be a New Testament to him who comes with a fresh desire of information. . . . How fruitful are the seeming barren places of Scripture. Bad ploughmen, which make balks of such ground. Wheresoever the surface of God's Word doth not laugh and sing with corn, there the heart thereof within is merry with mines, affording, where not plain matter, hidden mysteries."—FULLER, *Good Thoughts in Bad Times.*

beneath all the texts, and a jet from that fiery sea comes up and burns on the surface.

We are too easily satisfied with enjoying isolated texts. The shock and stimulus which a single text can give is very valuable, but a whole book of Scripture can give a far more powerful shock, if we read it from beginning to end and try to grasp its message as a whole. From this we may advance to groups of books. Sometimes we might take a single subject and go through the whole Bible to find out what is taught on it. And why should we not at last make the attempt to grasp all that the Bible has to teach, for faith on the one hand and for conduct on the other?

The best guide to the fulness of Scripture is to search it, as Jesus did, as the chart of our own life. In a different way, indeed, from that in which He found His life prefigured there, yet in a perfectly legitimate way, we shall find the exact form and image of our own. In precept and promise and example we shall see every deed we have to do, every resolution we have to form, every turn in life we have to take, laid down; and, if we act as it is written, we shall be able to follow up what we do by saying, as He so often did, "This has been done that the Scripture might be fulfilled."

Such a course earnestly followed will, however, bring us still nearer to His method of studying the Scriptures; for it will inevitably land us in the great central current which runs through the whole of Scripture from first to last. What is this? It is nothing but Christ Himself. The whole stream and drift of the Old Testament moves straight to the cross of Christ. The whole New Testament is nothing but the portrait of Christ. Let a man seek the true course of his own life in the Word, and inevitably it will land him at the cross, to seek mercy as a perishing sinner in the Saviour's wounds; and let him, starting afresh from this point of departure, seek his true course still farther, and inevitably what he will see will be, rising upon him in the distance, astonishing and enchaining him, but drawing him ever on, the image of perfection in the man Christ Jesus.

IX.

Christ as a Worker

Matt.	iv. 24.
	viii. 16, 17.
	ix. 35.
	xi. 1, 4, 5.
	xii. 15.
	xiii. 2.
	xiv. 13, 14, 35, 36.
	xv. 30.
	xix. 1, 2.
Mark	ii. 2.
	iii. 20.
	vi. 31, 54-56.
	xiii. 34.
	xiv. 8.
Luke	vi. 19.
	x. 2.
	xii. 1.
	xiii. 32, 33.
John	ii. 4.
	iv. 32-34.
	vii. 6, 8.
	ix. 4.
	xii. 23.
	xvii. 4.
	xix. 30.

CHAPTER IX.

Christ as a Worker.

There are two ideals as to work—the one to do as little, and the other to do as much, as possible. The former may be called the Oriental, the latter the Occidental, ideal. The child of the East, living in a warm climate, where movement or exertion soon tires, counts idleness the height of enjoyment, and passes his time, if he can, in a lazy dream. His very clothing is an index of his tastes— the capacious garment, the loose slipper. The son of the West, on the contrary, is apt to be a stirring being; he likes the excitement of endeavour and the exultation of achievement. His clothing is the least elegant in the world, but it has one virtue which in his eyes is a sufficient compensation: it is suitable for movement and work. His very pastimes are strenuous: whilst the Oriental after work stretches himself on a divan, the Briton spends his leisure in football or hunting.

Even in the West, indeed, there are great differences in the tastes of individuals. People of lethargic temperament are slow to work and prone to laziness, whilst those of the choleric temperament sometimes carry the enthusiasm for exertion to such extremes that they do not feel right unless they are in a kind of tempest of occupation. Among certain classes the goal of ambition is to be in a position to be able, if you choose, to do nothing; this is called being a gentleman. But the shrewder heads perceive that the pleasures of such a position, when it is won, seldom come up to the expectations of its possessor, unless, when released from a bread-winning calling, he voluntarily devotes himself to some of those invaluable services to the community or the Church which the leisured can best discharge, and on which the welfare of modern society so much depends.

Such are the differences which prevail amongst men when choosing only according to taste or temperament; but on this subject, as elsewhere, our Lord has set before us, in His teaching and example, the will of God.

I.

In its bearing on this question there is endless significance in the fact that Jesus was born in the cottage of a working man and spent the greater part of His life doing the work of a village carpenter. It is impossible to believe that this happened by chance; for the minutest circumstances of the life of Christ must have been ordered by God. The Jews expected the Messiah to be a prince; but God decreed that He should be born a working man. And so Jesus built the cottages of the villagers of Nazareth, constructed the waggon of the farmer, and mended perhaps the plaything of the child.

This sheds immortal honour upon work. The Greeks and the Romans despised manual labour, accounting it only fit for slaves; and this pagan notion easily slips back into the minds of men. But the example of the Son of man will always protect the dignity of honest labour; and the heart of the artisan will sing at his work as he remembers that Jesus of Nazareth stood at the bench and handled the tools of the carpenter.

The virtue of work is manifold. It stamps the brute earth and the raw materials taken out of it with the signature of mind,* which is the image and superscription of Him who is the Supreme

---

* Compare Schleiermacher's definition of Ethics, as "the Collective operation of active human reason upon nature," and of the aim of moral effort as "the perfect inter-penetration of reason and nature, a permeation of nature by reason." —WUTTKE, *Christian Ethics*, vol. i., p. 48 (translation).

Reason. It is a contribution to the happiness of the race, and it brings the individual into co-operation with all his fellow-creatures in the common task of taking possession of their habitation. It reacts too on the worker. It is a daily school of patience, sympathy and honesty. The man who scamps his work degrades himself.

Our age has learnt these truths well, because they have been expounded to it by several of its favourite and wisest teachers; and there is no healthier element in the literature of our century than this Gospel of Labour, as it is called. It has taught many a man to do his work thoroughly, not merely because he is paid for it, but because he delights in it for its own sake and respects himself too much to pass off for work what he knows to be sham.*

II.

Although the commonest work well done is honourable, every kind of work is not of equal honour. There are some callings in which a man can contribute far more directly and amply than in others to the welfare of his fellow-creatures, and these stand highest in the scale of honour.

It was on this principle that Jesus acted when He quitted the bench of the carpenter to devote Himself to preaching and healing. Than these two there are no callings more honourable, the

---

* "'Who draws a line and satisfies his soul,
Making it crooked where it should be straight?
An idiot with an oyster-shell may draw
His lines along the sand, all wavering,
Fixing no point or pathway to a point;
An idiot one remove may choose his line,
Straggle and be content; but, God be praised,
Antonio Stradivari has an eye
That winces at false work and loves the true,
With hand and arm that play upon the tool
As willingly as any singing bird
Sets him to sing his morning roundelay,
Because he likes to sing and likes the song.
Then Naldo: 'Tis a petty kind of fame
At best, that comes of making violins;
And saves no masses, either. Thou wilt go
To purgatory none the less.'

one ministering directly to the soul and the other to the body. By adopting them, however, Jesus stamped a fresh dignity on the work both of the preacher and of the physician; and, ever since, many in both professions have gone about their duties with intenser ardour and enjoyment because they have been conscious of walking in His footsteps.

But, though His work had changed, He was not less a worker than He had been before. It is a common theme of discussion between manual and professional labourers whether the toil of the hand or that of the brain is the more severe. The artisan thinks that his well-clothed neighbour, who does not need to touch rough materials or lift heavy loads, has an easy time of it; whilst the professional man, harassed with anxiety and responsibility, sighs for the regular hours, the well learnt task and the freedom from care of the working man. This is a controversy which will never be decided. But it is certain, in the case of Jesus at least, that it was when He entered on His new career that the real hard work of His life began. His three years of work as preacher and healer were years of unexampled toil. Wherever He went multitudes followed Him; when He went into any new region, they sent into all the country round about and brought unto Him all that were diseased in mind or body; the crowds about Him sometimes swelled to such dimensions that the people trode one upon

---

But he:
"'Twere purgatory here to make them ill;
And for my fame—when any master holds,
'Twixt chin and band a violin of mine,
He will be glad that Stradivari lived,
Made violins, and made them of the best.
The masters only know whose work is good:
They will choose mine; and, while God gives them skill,
I give them instruments to play upon,
God choosing me to help Him.'

'What! were God
At fault for violins, thou absent?'

'Yes;
He were at fault for Stradivari's work.'"

GEORGE ELIOT *Stradivarius.*

another; and sometimes He had not time even to eat. Such was the pressure and congestion of work with which He was beset. It is the kind of life which many have to live in this busy age; but we can look to Jesus and see in what spirit to carry the burden.

III.

In Christ's teaching there are many sayings on the responsibility of devoting our time and strength to the work of the world. We are servants, to every one of whom the Divine Taskmaster has given his own work; and, when He returns, He will rigidly require an account of whether or not it has been done.

The most solemn utterance of this kind is the great parable of the talents. The master, going into a far country, leaves each of his servants with a certain amount of money, one with more, another with less; it is to be well employed in his absence; and, when he comes back, he looks to receive not only the principal, but the additional money it has gained. Those who have made use of their trust diligently enter into the joy of their lord; but the servant who has done nothing with his talent is cast into outer darkness. It is a parable of truly awful solemnity. It evidently means that at the last judgment God will expect us to produce work done equivalent to the talents and opportunities He has conferred upon us; and merely to have done nothing with them, as the man with one talent did, will be enough to condemn us. It is not necessary to waste our time and squander our strength, money and other gifts on bad objects: merely to have failed to expend them on the work of life will incur the extreme penalty of the law.*

---

* "And who art thou that braggest of thy life of Idleness; complacently showest thy bright gilt equipages; sumptuous cushions; appliances for folding of the hands to mere sleep? Looking up, looking down, around, behind or before, discernest thou, if it be not in Mayfair alone, any *idle* hero, saint, god, or even devil? Not a vestige of one. In the Heavens, in the Earth, in the Waters under the Earth, is none like unto thee. Thou art an original figure in this Creation; a denizen in Mayfair alone, in this extraordinary Century or Half-Century alone! One monster there is in the world: the idle man. What is his 'Religion'? That Nature is

This is an exceedingly severe view of life; but it is the view by which Jesus lived Himself. He did not preach what He did not practise. He was doubtless conscious of possessing vast powers and of being capable of exerting an influence which would produce enormous changes both on individuals and in history. But the time allowed Him for putting this influence forth and impressing it on the world was very brief. He knew this, and He always acted like one who has a great work to do and little time to do it. Every hour of His time seemed to be apportioned to its own part of the task, for, when asked to do anything sooner than He intended, He would say, "Mine hour is not yet come." Everything with Him had its own hour. This made Him bold in the face of danger, for He knew that He was immortal till His work was done. As He said, there are twelve hours in the day of a human life, and, till these are spent, a man walks in safety beneath the shield of Providence. The edge of earnestness on His spirit grew keener as time went on; the purpose of life burned more within Him, and He was straitened till it should be accomplished. On His last journey to Jerusalem, as He went before His disciples in the way, "they were amazed, and, as they followed, they were afraid." "I must work the work of Him that sent Me," He would say, "while it is day; the night cometh, when no man can work."

IV.

There is intense joy in work when it is done and well done. The humblest mechanic feels this pleasure, when he sees the article he has been making passing out of his hands perfect. The

---

a Phantom, where cunning beggary or thievery may sometimes find good victual. That God is a lie; and that Man and his life are a lie.—Alas, alas, who of us *is* there that can say, I have worked? The faithfullest of us are unprofitable servants; the faithfullest of us know that best. The faithfullest of us may say, with sad and true old Samuel, 'Much of my life has been trifled away!' But he that has, and except 'on public occasions' professes to have, no function but that of going idle in a graceful or graceless manner, and of begetting sons to go idle; . . . on what iron spikes is he rushing?"—CARLYLE, *Past and Present*.

On this subject the professional philosophers are no less severe. See DORNER, *Christliche Sittenlehre*, p. 460.

poet surely feels it when he writes Finis at the end of the work into which he has poured the full force of his genius. What must it have been to William Wilberforce to hear on his deathbed that the cause to which he had devoted the toil of a lifetime had triumphed, and to know that, when he died, there would not be a single slave breathing in any of the dependencies of Britain!

Jesus drank deeply of this well of pleasure. The work He was doing was done perfectly at every stage; and it was work of the most beneficent and enduring kind. As He saw part after part of it falling accomplished behind Him, as He saw hour after hour receding into the past filled with its God-appointed work, He whispered to Himself, "My meat is to do the will of Him that sent Me, and to finish His work." And in the article of death, as He saw the last fold of the grand design unrolled, He passed out of the world with the cry on His lips, "It is finished!" He uttered this cry as a soldier might do on the battlefield, who perceives, with the last effort of consciousness, that the struggle in which he has sacrificed his life has been a splendid victory. But the triumph and the reward of His work never come to an end; for still, as the results of what He did unfold themselves age after age, as His words sink deeper into the minds of men, as His influence changes the face of the world, and as heaven fills with those whom He has redeemed, "He shall see of the travail of His soul, and shall be satisfied."

V.

Rest is as necessary a part of life as work. Even for work's sake it is necessary; for it restores the worker to himself, putting him in possession of all his powers and enabling him to do his best.

Jesus knew how to rest as well as how to work. Though there was constant haste in His life, there was no hurry; though there was much pressure, there was no confusion. Nothing was more conspicuous in Him than His unvarying dignity, calmness and self-possession.

He never did anything unprepared. As He never did anything before the time, so He never did anything after it. One-half of the worry and confusion of life arises from doing things at the wrong time, the mind being either weakened by borrowing to-day the trouble of to-morrow or exhausted by having on hand not only to-day's work but that which ought to have been done yesterday. God never wants us to do more in a day than we have time for; and the day will be found to have room enough for its own work if it is not encumbered with the work of the day past or the care of the day to come.*

Jesus was ready for every duty because He came up with it strengthened by the perfect discharge of the duty preceding it. His work in the carpenter's shop was a preparation for the work of preaching. It acquainted Him with human nature and human life, initiating Him especially into the joys and sorrows of the poor, to whom it was afterwards His boast to preach. Many a preacher misses the mark because, though he knows books, he does not know men. But Jesus "knew what was in man, and needed not that any should teach Him." He did not quit this school of experience till He was thirty years of age. Eager as He must have been for the work which lay before Him, He did not rush into it prematurely, but waited hidden in the country, till mind and body were mature and everything fully ripe; and then He came forth travelling in the greatness of His strength and did His work swiftly, surely, perfectly.

But in the midst of His work also He took means to preserve His independence and peace of mind. When the multitude pressing on Him grew too large and stayed too long, He withdrew Himself into the wilderness. Neither the desire to go on preaching nor even the appeals of the sick and dying could detain Him when He felt He needed to preserve His own calmness and self-

---

* "Æsthetically we may say that want of time is want of genius; for genius accomplishes in a very short time, and in right time, what others cannot accomplish in an unlimited time. But ethically expressed, it is this: want of time is want of moral energy and wisdom."—MARTENSEN, *General Ethics*, p. 426.

possession. After days of too crowded work He would disappear, to refresh His body by casting it on the breast of nature and His soul by casting it on the bosom of God. When He saw His disciples becoming exhausted or excited, He would say, "Come ye yourselves apart into a desert place and rest a while." For even in the holiest work it is possible to lose oneself. One may resign oneself so completely to the appeals and needs of men as to have no leisure for communion with God. The enthusiastic minister, consumed with zeal and willing to please everybody, neglects his study and allows his mind to become starved; and the result is inevitable. He becomes stale, flat and unprofitable; and those whose importunities have induced him to sacrifice his true self are the first to turn round and complain that he has disappointed them.

For the great mass of the world's workers the principal opportunity of rest is the Sabbath.* Jesus threw His shield over this institution, maintaining that it was made for man, and therefore none had the right to take it from him. In His day those who tried to take it away were the Pharisees, who converted it from a day of

---

* "The importance to a statesman of refusing to be hurried was recognised by Talleyrand. He had drawn up a confession of faith, which was to be sent to the Pope on the day of his death. On the day before he died he was supposed to be at the point of death, and he was asked whether the paper should be sent off. His reply was addressed to the Duchesse de Dino, who repeated it to the first Lord Ashburton, from whom I heard it: I '*Attendez jusqu'à demain. Toute ma vie je me suis fait une règle de ne jamais me presser, et j'ai toujours été à temps.*'

"With a view to promote thorough calmness, orderliness,—and with higher views also, though these have respect to the man rather than exclusively to the statesman,—it were to be wished that he should set apart from business, not only a sabbatical day in each week, but, if it be possible, a sabbatical hour in each day. I do not here refer to his devotional exercises exclusively, but to the advantage he may derive from quitting the current of busy thoughts, and cutting out for himself in each day a sort of cell for reading or meditation—a space resembling one of those Lights or incurvations in the course of a rapid stream (called by the Spaniards resting-places), where the waters seem to tarry and repose themselves for a while. This, if it were only by exercising the statesman's powers of self-government—of intention and remission in business, of putting the mind on and taking it off—would be a practice well paid; for it is to these powers that he must owe his exemption from the dangers to mind, body, and

sacred delight into a day set with thorns to wound the conscience. This danger is not yet past; but in our day the attack comes more from the other side—from the Sadducees rather than the Pharisees. The movements against the Sabbath originate at present almost entirely with the idle rich, who naturally, after spending six days in a round of pleasure and dissipation, have no taste for a day of quietness, when they might have to look within and face themselves. If they obeyed the first part of the fourth commandment, "Six days shalt thou labour," they would have more comprehension of the second. They generally profess, indeed, to be acting in the interest of the poor; but they take the name of the poor in vain, for the poor know better. They know that, wherever the sacredness of the Sabbath is overridden, the poor man has seven days to toil instead of six. Wherever the continental Sunday prevails, the noise of mill and foundry is heard on Sabbath as well as Saturday; and, should the working classes of this country ever yield to a movement for secularising the Lord's Day, they will find it true that, whilst they that honour God are honoured, those who despise Him shall be lightly esteemed.

It is, however, a problem always requiring fresh consideration, as the conditions of life change, how to observe the Sabbath. The day of rest is not rightly spent unless it is a delight to man as well as holiness to the Lord. But surely the best security for reaping all the fruits it was intended to yield is to spend it in the spirit and the company of Him after whom it is called the Lord's Day.

---

business of continued nervous excitement. But to a statesman of a high order of intellect such intermissions of labour will yield a further profit; they will tend to preserve in him some remains of such philosophic or meditative faculties as may be crumbling under the shocks and pressures of public life. One who shall have been deeply imbued in his early years with the love of meditative studies, will find that in any such hour of tranquillity which he shall allow himself, the recollection of them will spring up in his mind with a light and spiritual emanation, in like manner (to resume the similitude) as a bubble of air springs from the bottom of the stayed waters."—Sir Henry Taylor, *The Statesman*, pp, 275, 276.

X.

Christ as a Sufferer

Matt.   ii. 13-18.
iv. 1.
viii. 16, 17, 20.
ix. 3.
xi. 19.
xii. 24.
xiii. 54-58.
xvi. 21.
xvii. 22, 23.
xx. 17-19.
xxvi.
xxvii.

Mark   iii. 21, 22.
viii. 17-21.
ix. 19.
xiv. 50.

Luke   iv. 28, 29.
vi. 7.
xi. 53, 54.
xvi. 14.

John   vi. 66.
vii. 7, 12; 19, 20; 32, 52.
ix. 16, 22, 29.
x. 20.
xii. 10, 11, 27.
xv. 18.
xvii. 14.
xviii. 22.

CHAPTER X.

Christ as a Sufferer.

I.

Work is but one half of life; suffering is the other. There is a hemisphere of the world in the sunshine of work, but there is another in the shadow of suffering.

Not, indeed, that in any life these states alternate with anything like the same regularity with which the earth rolls out of darkness into light, and back again from light into darkness. Nothing is more mysterious than the proportions in which the two elements are distributed in different lots. Some enjoy the exhilaration of successful exertion nearly all their days, and know little or nothing of illness, bereavement or defeat. Others appear to be marked out by suffering for its own. All through life they are "acquainted with grief;" they are scarcely ever out of mourning, because ever and anon death is knocking at their door to claim their dearest; their own health is precarious; and, whatever dreams of high and sustained achievement may visit them, they know, as soon as the excitement subsides, that they have not physical strength to carry out their vision.

If you are a child of fortune, scarcely ever knowing a day's ill health and delighting in your work, whose results you see day by day waxing greater and more imposing behind you, go and stand by the bedside of an invalid laid down with incurable disease.

There you may recognise a mind more capable than your own, a heart as fit as yours for love and enjoyment; but an invisible chain is wound round the limbs and holds them fast; and, though the martyrdom may last for ten or twenty years, that figure will never rise with its own strength from where it lies. What does your philosophy make of such a sight ? Yet it is only an extreme instance of what is occurring in a thousand forms. The children of sorrow are numerous, and no man knows how soon his own life of work may be changed into a life of suffering. Any moment a bolt may break from the blue and alter everything. A cloud no bigger than a man's hand may wax and spread till it drapes the sky in blackness from horizon to horizon. And, even if no such awful calamity come, time brings to all their own share of suffering.

> There is no flock, however watched and tended,
> But one dead lamb is there;
> There is no household, howsoe'er defended,
> But has one vacant chair.

Suffering, then, is not an element of life that can be ignored. If we need one to show us how to work, not less do we need one to teach us how to suffer. And here, again, the Son of man does not fail us. Whilst He is the great Captain of work, calling out the young and the energetic to dare and to achieve, He is also the sufferer's Friend, round whom are gathered the weak, the disappointed and the agonized. When on the cross He cried, "It is finished," He was referring not only to the work of His life successfully accomplished, but also to the cup of suffering drunk out to the last drop.

II.

1. Jesus suffered from what may be called the ordinary privations of humanity. He was born in a stable and laid in a manger, thus at the very outset of His career stepping into the dark hemisphere of suffering. We know little of the social condition in which He was brought up: we cannot tell whether or not in Mary's home He dwelt much in the shadow of want and misfor-

tune. But at a later stage, we know from Himself, "foxes had holes and the birds of the air had nests, but the Son of man had not where to lay His head." It is not often that one of the children of men is reduced so low as thus to have to envy the beast its lair and the bird its nest. As a rule the end of human life, when the habitation in which the soul has tabernacled is broken up, is attended with more or less of suffering; but the physical suffering which He endured at the last was extreme. We need only recall the bloody sweat of Gethsemane; the scourging, when His body, bent over a short post, was beaten with all the force of cruel soldiers; the thrusting of the crown of thorns on His head; the complicated tortures of crucifixion. We may not be able to assert that none ever suffered so much physical agony as He, but this is at least probable; for the exquisiteness of His physical organism in all likelihood made Him much more sensitive than others to pain.

2. He suffered keenly from the pain of anticipating coming evil. When great sorrow or pain comes on suddenly, there is sometimes a kind of bewilderment in it which acts as an anodyne, and it may be over before the sufferer thoroughly realises it. But to know that one is in the grasp of a disease which in, say, six months will develop into intolerable agony before carrying one away, fills the mind with a horror of anticipation which is worse than even the reality when it comes. Jesus foreknew His sufferings and foretold them to His disciples; and these communications grew more and more vivid and minute month by month, as if they were taking ever stronger hold of His imagination. This horror of anticipation culminated in Gethsemane; for it was the dread of what was coming which there produced in His mind such a tumult of amazement and agony that the sweat fell like great blood-drops from His face.

3. He suffered from the sense of being the cause of suffering to others. To persons of an unselfish disposition the keenest pang inflicted by their own weakness or misfortunes may sometimes be to see those whom they would like to make happy rendered miserable through connection with themselves. To the child Jesus

how gruesome must have been the story of the babes of Bethlehem, whom the sword of Herod smote when it was seeking for Him! Or, if His mother spared Him this recital, He must at least have learned how she and Joseph had to flee with Him to Egypt to escape the jealousy of Herod. As His life drew near its close, this sense that connection with Himself might be fatal to His friends forced itself more and more upon His notice. When He was arrested, He tried to protect the Twelve from His own fate, pleading with His captors, "Let these go their way." But He foresaw too clearly that the world which hated Him would hate them also, and, as He said, that the time would come when whosoever killed them would think that he was doing God service. He had to see the sword piercing the heart of His mother when she gazed up at Him dying a death more shameful in that age than death on the gallows is in ours.

4. The element of shame was all through a large ingredient in His cup of suffering. To a sensitive mind there is nothing more intolerable; it is far harder to bear than bodily pain. But it assailed Jesus in nearly every form, pursuing Him all through His life. He was railed at for the humbleness of His birth. The high-born priests and the educated rabbis sneered at the carpenter's son who had never learned, and the wealthy Pharisees derided Him. He was again and again called a madman. Evidently this was what Pilate took Him for; and, when He appeared before Herod, the gay monarch and his men of war "set Him at nought." The Roman soldiers adopted an attitude of savage banter towards Him all through His trial and crucifixion, treating Him as boys torment one who is weak in the mind. They spat in His face; they blindfolded Him, and then, smiting Him, asked, "Prophesy who struck thee!" They made Him a mock-king, with the cast-off coat of a soldier for a mantle, a reed for a sceptre, and the thorns for a crown. Under such indignities had His godlike mind to burn. He heard Barabbas preferred to Himself by the voice of His fellow-countrymen, and He was crucified between thieves, as if He were the worst of the worst. A hail of mockery kept falling on Him in His

dying hours. The passers-by made faces of derision at Him, adding with their lips the vilest insults; and even the thieves who were crucified with Him cast contempt in His teeth. Thus had He who was conscious of irresistible strength to submit to be treated as the weakest of weaklings, and He who was the Wisdom of the Highest to submit to be used as if He were less than a man.

5. But to Jesus it was more painful still, being the Holy One of God, to be regarded and treated as the chief of sinners. To one who loves God and goodness there can be nothing so odious as to be suspected of hypocrisy and to know that he is believed to be perpetrating crimes at the opposite extreme from his public profession. Yet this was what Jesus was accused of. He was believed to be in collusion with the powers of evil and to cast out devils by Beelzebub, the prince of the devils. He to whom the name of God was as ointment poured forth was called a blasphemer and a Sabbath-breaker. His very best acts were misconstrued; and for going to seek the lost where alone they could be found He had to submit to be called a glutton and a winebibber, a friend of publicans and sinners. In claiming to be the Messiah He was thought by the majority of all classes to be an unscrupulous pretender; the authorities, both ecclesiastical and secular, decided so in solemn court. Even His own disciples at last forsook Him; one of them betrayed Him; and the foremost of them all cursed and swore that he did not know Him. Possibly there was not a single human being, when He died, who believed that He was what He claimed to be.

6. If to the holy soul of Jesus it was painful to be believed to be guilty of sins which He had not committed, it must have been still more painful to feel that He was being thrust into sin itself. This attempt was often made.* Satan tried it in the wilderness,

---

* "Common usage, I cannot but think, has fallen into a serious error in speaking of the temptation in the wilderness. Men speak, if they do not think, as if this temptation stood alone in the life of Christ. Nothing can be a greater mistake. Our Lord's whole life was one continued temptation. We have but to read the memoirs, which the Holy Ghost has caused to be written for our learning,

and, although only this one temptation of his is detailed, he no doubt often returned to the attack. Wicked men tried it: they resorted to every device to cause Him to lose His temper and speak unadvisedly with His lips: "They began to urge Him vehemently, and to provoke Him to speak of many things, laying wait for Him and seeking to catch something out of His mouth." Even friends, who did not understand the plan of His life, endeavoured to divert Him from the course prescribed to Him by the will of God—so much so that He had once to turn on one of them, as if he were temptation personified, with "Get thee behind Me, Satan." Nothing could prove more clearly than such a saying, so unlike Him who uttered it, how keenly He felt the point of temptation, and what horror awoke in Him at the danger of transgressing by a hairsbreadth the will of God.

7. While the proximity of sin awoke such loathing in His holy soul, and the touch of it was to Him like the touch of fire on delicate flesh, He was brought into the closest contact with it, and hence arose His deepest suffering. It pressed its loathsome presence on Him from a hundred quarters. He who could not bear to look on it saw it in its worst forms close to His very eyes. His own presence in the world brought it out; for goodness stirs up the evil lying at the bottom of wicked hearts. The sacredness of the Person with whom they had to do intensified the virulence of Pharisees and Sadducees, and the crimes of Pilate and Judas. What a sea of all the evil passions in human nature He was gaz-

---

in order to recognise in almost every page how the Lord Jesus Christ was exposed to ceaseless temptations. He was subjected to trials of temper, trials of character, trials of principle; He was harassed by temptations caused by nervous irritability, or want of strength, or physical weakness, or bodily weariness; unfair opposition was constantly urging Him to give way to undue anger and unrestrained passion; or rejection and desertion would, had it been possible, have betrayed Him into moodiness or cynical despair. The machinations of His foes, the fickleness of the mob, even the foolishness of His disciples, were scarcely ever wanting to try His spirit, and would often goad Him beyond endurance. All the continually recurring trials, which are ever betraying man into faults he has bitterly to deplore, and into sins of which he has to repent in sorrow, were present in the life of the Lord Jesus Christ."—BERNARD, *The Mental Characteristics of the Lord Jesus Christ.*

ing over when, as He hung on the cross, His eye fell on the upturned faces of the multitude!

It was as if all the sin of the race were rushing upon Him, and Jesus felt as if it were all His own. In a large family of evildoers, where the father and mother are drunkards, the sons jail-birds and the daughters steeped in shame, there may be one, a daughter, pure, sensible, sensitive, living in the home of sin like a lily among thorns. And she makes all the sin of the family her own. The others do not mind it; the shame of their sin is nothing to them; it is the talk of the town, but they do not care. Only in her heart their crimes and disgrace meet like a sheaf of spears, piercing and mangling. The one innocent member of the family bears the guilt of all the rest. Even their cruelty to herself she hides, as if all the shame of it were her own. Such a position did Christ hold in the human family. He entered it voluntarily, becoming bone of our bone and flesh of our flesh; He identified Himself with it; He was the sensitive centre of the whole. He gathered into His heart the shame and guilt of all the sin He saw. The perpetrators did not feel it, but He felt it. It crushed Him; it broke His heart; and He died under the weight of the sin of others, which He had made His own.

Thus we try to bring home to our thoughts the mystery of Gethsemane and the awful cry of Golgotha, "My God, My God, why hast Thou forsaken Me?" But it is still a mystery. Who can draw near to that figure prostrate beneath the olive trees in the garden, or listen to that voice sounding from the cross, without feeling that there is a sorrow there whose depths we cannot fathom? We draw as near as we may, but something calls to us, "Hitherto shalt thou come, but no further." Only we know that it was sin which was crushing Him. "He was made sin for us who knew no sin, that we might be made the righteousness of God in Him."*

---

* George Herbert's *Sacrifice*, with its piercing refrain, "Was ever grief like Mine?" is too long to quote. It gives a detailed and most moving enumeration of the sources of the Saviour's sufferings.

III.

The Results of the sufferings of Christ are the principal theme of the Gospel; but only a few words on the subject can be said here.

1. The Epistle to the Hebrews says that "the Author of our salvation was made perfect through suffering;" and, again, that "He learned obedience through the things which He suffered."

These are mysterious statements. Was He imperfect that He needed to be made perfect, or disobedient that He required to learn obedience? They cannot surely mean that the smallest iota was ever wanting to complete His character in either sense. No, but simply because He was a man, with a human history and a human development, He had to ascend a stair, so to speak, of obedience and perfection, and, although every step was surmounted at its own precise time, and He emerged upon it perfect, yet every new step required a new effort and, when surmounted, brought Him to a higher stage of perfection and into a wider circle of obedience.* We see the progress of this effort with great clearness in Gethsemane, where in the first access of suffering He says, "Father, if it be possible, let this cup pass from Me;" but at the last is able to say in deep tranquillity, "O My Father, if this cup may not pass away from Me except I drink it, Thy will be done."

This was the perfection He attained through suffering. It was complete comprehension of the will of God and absolute harmony with it. This is our perfection too; and suffering is the great means of bringing it about: Many of us would never have thought much of God's will unless we had first felt it as a violent contra-

---

* "His divine nature was not unto Him in the place of a soul, nor did immediately operate the things which He performed, as some of old vainly imagined; but, being a perfect man, His rational soul was in Him the immediate principle of all His moral operations, even as ours are in us. Now, in the improvement and exercise of these faculties and powers of His soul, He had and made a progress after the manner of other men; for He was made like unto us 'in all things,' yet without sin. In their increase, enlargement, and exercise there was required a progression in grace also; and this He had continually by the Holy Ghost (Luke ii. 40)."—OWEN, *On the Holy Spirit.*

diction of our own. We wondered at it, and rebelled against it; but, when we learned, after Jesus, to say, "Not my will, but Thine, be done," we found that this is the secret of life, and the peace which passeth all understanding came into our souls. Or at least we have seen the process in others. I daresay to some of us the most priceless of all memories is that of one of the sons or daughters of affliction made beautiful by submission to the will of God. There had perhaps been a struggle once; but it was over; and God's will was accepted, not only with submission, but with a holy joy which glorified the whole being. And, as we have watched the pure and patient face on the pillow, we have felt that here was one who by surrender had won the victory, and we have confessed that our own life, with all its storm and stress of activity, might be far less valuable to either God or man than this one lying bound and motionless:

> They also serve who only stand and wait.

2. St Paul, in one of the most confidential passages of his writings, tells of a lesson which he learned from suffering. "Blessed be God," he says, "the Father of mercies and God of all comfort, who comforteth us in all our tribulation, that we may be able to comfort them which are in any trouble by the comfort wherewith we ourselves are comforted of God."* He was glad that he had suffered, because he had learned thereby how to deal with sufferers. How like his big heart was the sentiment! And it is profoundly true. Suffering gives the power to comfort. Indeed, there is no other way of acquiring the art. To one in deep trouble there is all the difference in the world between the words of the heart-whole, who have never themselves been in the fire, and the tender grasp and sympathetic tones of those who have personally suffered. Those, therefore, who are in the furnace of bereavement or pain may take to themselves the inspiring suggestion, Perhaps this is my apprenticeship to the sacred office of the comforter.

---

* 2 Cor. i. 3, 4.

Jesus thus acquired the art; and the tried and tempted of every generation come to Him with a confidence which is born of the knowledge of how He personally explored all the recesses of this kind of experience. "We have not an high priest which cannot be touched with the feeling of our infirmities, but was in all points tempted like as we are, yet without sin."

3. The results of the sufferings of Christ enter still more deeply into His work as the Saviour. He foresaw them Himself and spoke often about them. "Except a corn of wheat," He said, "fall into the ground and die, it abideth alone; but, if it die, it bringeth forth much fruit;" "I if I be lifted up from the earth, will draw all men unto Me;" "As Moses lifted up the serpent in the wilderness, even so must the Son of man be lifted up, that whosoever believeth on Him should not perish, but have eternal life."

When He died, His cause seemed to be lost. Not a single adherent was left clinging to it. But, when this eclipse was over and He came forth from the grave, His adherents awoke to discover that they possessed in Him a hundred times more than they had before been aware of; and the new glory in which He shone was that of the suffering Saviour.

In every age His sufferings attract to Him the hearts of men; for they prove the boundless extent of His love, His absolute unselfishness, and His loyalty to truth and principle even unto death. Thus they have power with men.

But they have also power with God. "He is the propitiation for our sins; and not for ours only, but also for the sins of the whole world." Because He died we need not die. God has put into His hands the forgiveness of sins to be bestowed as a free gift on all who receive Him. Because He humbled Himself God hath highly exalted Him. He is seated now at the right hand of power, a Prince and a Saviour, and He carries at His girdle the keys of hell and of death.

XI.

Christ as a Philanthropist

Matt.   iv. 23, 24.
         viii. 16, 17.
         ix. 35, 36.
         x. 1, 8.
         xi. 4, 5.
         xiv. 13, 14; 36.
         xv. 30-32.
         xix. 21.
         xxi. 14.
         xxv. 34-40.
         xxvi. 8-11.

Mark   vi. 54-56.
         x. 21.

Luke   x. 12-17.

John   xiii. 29.

CHAPTER XI.

Christ as a Philanthropist.

I.

Philanthropist may be thought too light a name to apply to Christ. And it must be confessed that it has a secular sound.

Some words are unfortunate: in common usage they are degraded, and their original meaning is lost. The word "charity" is a well-known instance. Originally meaning "love," it had at one time a good chance of being the technical term for the very highest kind of love—that passion which is kindled by union with Christ. This is its meaning in the thirteenth of First Corinthians, and the authority of so great a chapter might have been expected to determine for ever the usage of Christendom. But somehow the word missed this honour and suffered degradation; and now "charity" is another name for "alms." In like manner, "philanthropy" has been brought down by usage to denote work done on behalf of men's bodies and temporal condition, as distinguished from work done for their spiritual good. But originally it was not so restricted, but meant simply love to men.

In this wide sense it is ascribed in Scripture to God Himself. Thus, in a well-known passage in the Epistle to Titus, the literal rendering is, "But after that the kindness and philanthropy* of

---

* A.V., "love of God our Saviour towards man."

God our Saviour appeared, not by works of righteousness which we have done, but according to His mercy He saved us, by the washing of regeneration and renewing of the Holy Ghost, which He shed on us abundantly through Jesus Christ our Saviour." Here it will be perceived, philanthropy denotes, not God's kindness to the bodies of men, but His grace to their souls; for it displayed itself in bestowing the washing of regeneration and the renewing of the Holy Ghost.

It was in the same way that the philanthropy of Christ also primarily manifested itself, His work and sufferings being gone through with a view in the first place to the salvation of men's souls, while the relief of their bodily wants and ailments came in only in the second place. Nor is it easy to understand why work done for the soul's sake should not be called philanthropy as much as work for the body's. From the Christian standpoint at least it is a far greater kindness; and none can deny that it often involves far-reaching temporal advantages. In both foreign and home missions the success of the Gospel, when it saves men's souls, generally includes, as a secondary but inevitable accompaniment, the sweeping away of masses of cruelty, poverty and ignorance.

If, indeed, the improvement of men's temporal condition be dignified with the name of philanthropy, and sharply dissociated from spiritual aims, the name of Philanthropist must be denied to Jesus. He unfolded the utmost consideration for the physical necessities of men, but always in subordination to the higher wants of the soul. His love extended to the whole man—body and soul together. His love to God and His love to man were not two passions, but one. He loved man because He saw God in him—God's handiwork, God's image, the object of God's love.

This must ever be the pulse of a powerful philanthropy—to see God in man; or, as Christians more naturally phrase it, to see Christ in man. "Inasmuch as ye did it unto the least of these ye did it unto Me," are Christ's own words. When I touch the body of a man, I am touching what was made to be a temple of the Holy

Ghost. In the humblest—ay, in the most sinful—human being we see one whom God loves, whom the Saviour died for, and who may be an heir of the glory of Christ. These are the deep wells of conviction out of which a strong philanthropy is nourished.

II.

It cannot be said that an active philanthropy has always been a characteristic of those professing godliness. Jesus Himself gave a significant hint of this in the Parable of the Good Samaritan. The priest and the Levite passed the poor maltreated way-farer by, whereas the milk of human kindness was found in the common, unordained man. History supplies too many instances to confirm the parable. Often has the untrained heart of humanity noted and branded a wrong, and the uncovenanted hand sprung forth to the relief of misery, when those expressly called by their offices to the service have remained silent and supine. It would even seem sometimes as if intense sympathy with God destroyed sympathy with man. But one of the greatest services of Jesus to the world was to harmonize religion and morality. He would not allow neglect of man to be covered by zeal for God, but ever taught that he only loves God who loves his brother also.

At present we see these things, which He joined, put asunder from the other side. One of the novelties of our own age is an atheistic philanthropy. There are those who do not believe in God or the God-man, or in the spiritual and eternal world, but yet make a life of sacrifice for others the sum of morality. They confess that it was Jesus who brought their ideal into the world, and that it was established in the convictions of mankind by His authority; but now, they maintain, it is able to dispense with His support, and they call on us to love man, not for Christ's sake, but for his own. They profess to see in man himself, apart from God, enough to inspire hourly and life-long effort on his behalf; and in the very brevity of his existence, which comes completely to an end at death, they find a pathetic motive for instant activity, because he must be helped now or never.

In so far as any may be induced by such motives to embrace the life of self-denial and really grapple with the problems of poverty and crime, Christians need not hesitate to wish them God-speed. This is a wide world, affording room for experiments; and it is a world of such fearful misery that there is little need to forbid anyone who from any motive may feel inclined to lend it a helping hand. We may even recognise some to be for Christ who believe themselves to be against Him. But, where the opposition is radical and final, we are hardly justified either by reason or the facts of the case in expecting very much from such a movement.

No doubt there is in the natural heart a love of man for man, which, if blown up by a favourable wind, may now and then do wonders; and the kindness of those who make no profession of religion sometimes puts Christians to shame. But, on the other hand, the force which the philanthropic spirit has to overcome is one of the mightiest in nature. It is the force of selfishness—that universally diffused instinct which makes the individual seek his own interest and happiness whatever comes of others, which makes the strong domineer over the weak and the many tyrannize over the few. This force lodges in every human breast; it pervades communities as well as individuals; it is embodied in customs and laws; it evolves new forms of wrong in every age; and many would say that it rules the world. This is the force which philanthropy has to overcome. It is not easily dislodged. It will not be conquered by fine words. There is needed, to overcome it, a change which only God can work by communicating to us His own nature, which is love.

> 'Is there a reason in nature for these hard hearts?' O Lear,
> That a reason out of nature must turn them soft seems clear.

In the teaching of Christ man is so dignified by his connection with God and by his immortal destiny, that everyone who really believes this creed must feel himself condemned if he treats his brother ill. But strip man, as Agnosticism does, of all the greatness and mystery with which Christianity invests him—cease to believe that he comes from God, that he is akin to beings greater than himself who care for him, and that his soul is of infinite worth because it has before it an unending development—and how long will it be possible to cherish for him the reverence which wins him consideration and help? The brevity of man's existence gives him, according to the present teaching of Agnosticism, a pathetic claim to instant help; but who knows whether in a society given over to unbelief the argument might not tell the other way, the selfish heart reasoning that sufferings which must end so soon do not matter?

It was in the generation preceding the French Revolution that atheistic philanthropy took its rise. The prophets of the time were predicting an age of peace and brotherhood, when selfish passion should disappear and cruelty and wrong no more vex the world. But, when their teaching had done its work, its fruit appeared in the Revolution itself, whose unspeakable inhumanities afforded our race such glances into the dark depths of its own nature as can never be forgotten. It is painful to recall that Rousseau himself, the most eloquent and, in some respects, the noblest apostle of the new faith, while preaching universal brotherhood, sent his own children one by one, as they were born, to the Foundling Hospital, to save himself the trouble and expense of their support. The Revolution did much destructive work for which the hour had come; but it was a gigantic proof that the love necessary for the work of reconstruction must be sought in a superhuman source.*

---

* "The practical paradox, that the age in which the claims of humanity were most strongly asserted is also the age in which human nature was reduced to its lowest terms,—that the age of tolerance, philanthropy, and enlightenment was also the age of materialism, individualism, and scepticism,—is explicable only if we remember that both equally spring out of the negative form taken by the first assertion of human freedom.

"As the individual thus fell back upon himself, throwing off all relations to that which seemed to be external, the specific religious and social ideas of earlier days lost power over him; and their place was taken by the abstract idea of God and the abstract idea of the equality and fraternity of men,—ideas which seemed to be higher and nobler because they were more general, but which for

We are living at present in a state of society in which there is an after-glow of Christian sentiment even in minds that have ceased to name the name of Christ, which develops beautiful manifestations; but those who know human nature will demand very strictly where Agnosticism is to get the light and the glow which will keep back the on-rushing force of dark and selfish passion, when Christianity is removed. There is a remnant of Christianity in many who think they have got quit of it; but it remains to be seen how long this will last when cut off from its source. A sheet of ice holding on to the edges of a pool may maintain its position even after the water on whose surface it has been formed has been drawn off; but it will not maintain it long, and it will not bear much weight. The facts with which philanthropy has to deal are excessively disagreeable to face, and the temptations to spare oneself and enjoy the world are insistent. Not long ago, when the bitter cry of outcast London grew so piercing as to attract universal attention, the heart of the West End was stirred, and the sons and daughters of fashion left their frivolities to go "slumming," as it was called, in the East End. But already, I am told, this is nearly all over; and the work of relieving the wretched is left, for the most part, to the humble followers of Christ, who were at it before. If strict inquiry were made, I imagine it would be found that there are very few philanthropic institutions of any dimensions in our midst that would not go down if

---

that very reason were emptied of all definite meaning, as well as of all vital power to hold in check the lusts and greeds of man's lower nature. Thus the ambitious but vague proclamation of the religion of nature and the rights of man was closely associated with a theory which was reducing man to a mere animal individual, a mere subject of sensations and appetites, incapable either of religion or of morality. For an ethics which is more than a word, and a religion which is more than an aspiration, imply *definite* relations of men to each other and to God, and all such relations were now rejected as inconsistent with the freedom of the individual. The French Revolution was the practical demonstration that the mere general idea of religion is not a religion, and that the mere general idea of a social unity is not a state; but that such abstractions, inspiring as they may be as weapons of attack upon the old system, leave nothing behind to build up the new one, except the unchained passions of the natural man."
—E. CAIRD, *Hegel*, pp. 19, 20.

they were deprived of the support of those who give not only for the sake of man, but for the sake of the Saviour who has redeemed them.

III.

The actual forms in which the philanthropy of Christ manifested itself were mainly two.

One of these was the giving of alms to the poor. This was, it is evident, a constant habit of His—so much so, that when, on the night of the betrayal, He said to Judas, who had the bag, "That thou doest do quickly," the rest of the disciples thought that the message the betrayer had received was to visit and relieve with a gift of money someone in distress. How the bag was filled we do not know very well. Jesus may have put into it savings of His own which He had laid by, when working as a carpenter, in view of the life He had in prospect. The Twelve may have done the same; and the holy women who followed Him contributed to it. But there is no reason to think that it was ever very full, but the contrary. When Jesus gave alms, it was the poor giving to the poor; yet He kept up the practice to the very end.

There have been good men who have seen so much peril in this form of philanthropy that they have pronounced against it altogether; but the example of Jesus supports it. There can be no doubt, however, that it requires caution and consideration. To give to the professional beggar generally does more harm than good, and too facile yielding to his importunities is to be accounted a vice rather than a virtue.* But there are deserving poor. They are known to those whose work lies among them; and the wealthy might with advantage make these workers their almoners. But it is not difficult to find them out, if we are willing to go on our own feet into the abodes of poverty. To many,

---

*Compare DORNER, *Christliche Sittenlehre*, p. 469: "There is something holy in poverty. The poor are the altar of the Church. But there is no holiness in beggary."

indeed, this is an unexplored world, though it is at their doors. But it is not difficult to discover. Once enter it with a loving heart, and progress is easy. You will find in it honest men, on whom illness or temporary want of work has fallen, and whom a gift may help honourably over the time of need. You will find the aged, who have fought the battle manfully, but now can fight no more; and surely it is an honour to have a few of these dependent on our bounty. Among the poorest there are princes of God, who at a future stage of existence may be in a position to patronise us.*

The other form of His philanthropy was healing. Because He healed by miracle we naturally think of it as easily done; but perhaps it was more an effort than we suppose. On one occasion, when a woman touched Him and was healed, without wishing Him to know, He did know, because, it is said, He perceived that virtue had gone out of Him. And there are other indications that these cures must have cost Him an expenditure of nervous sympathy and emotion which imparts a deep pathos to the saying of St. Matthew, "Himself took our infirmities and bare our sicknesses." But, in any case, the work of healing was a congenial one in which His loving nature rejoiced; and He was never more at home than in a crowd composed of persons suffering from every kind of disease and infirmity of body and mind, amongst whom He moved benignly, touching one here into health, speaking to another the word of power, and letting glances of kindness and good cheer fall on all. The joy radiated far and wide, when the father returned to his home to be no longer its burden but its bread-winner, the son to be no more a care but a pride, the mother to resume the place and the work from which illness had dis-

---

* "Those are ripe for charity who are withered by age or impotency,—especially if maimed in following their calling; for such are industry's martyrs, at least her confessors. Add to these those that with diligence fight against poverty, though neither conquer till death make it a drawn battle. Expect not, but prevent, their craving of thee; for God forbid the heavens should never rain till the earth first opens her mouth, seeing some grounds will sooner burn than chap!

"The House of Correction is the fittest hospital for those cripples whose legs are lame through their own laziness."—FULLER, *The Holy and Profane State.*

lodged her. The best help to the poor and needy is that which enables them to help themselves; and this was the kind of help which Jesus gave by His miracles.

We of course do not possess miraculous powers; but in their place we have others, which may be put to the like uses and are capable of working wonders as far beyond what could be achieved in His day through natural causes as His miracles are beyond us.

We possess, for instance, the power of science. There is no form of philanthropy perhaps more Christ-like than that which puts at the disposal of the poor and the ignorant first-rate medical skill. Our infirmaries and dispensaries are the continuation of Christ's healing activity. Medical missionaries carry to the heathen a commission singularly like that with which Jesus sent forth the apostles. The Church is beginning to employ trained nurses in mission work. And in every part of the country there are medical men who are daily rendering to the poorest the best efforts of their art, for which they receive little or no remuneration, but which they give with even greater inward delight than they feel in working for their best-paying patients, because they are serving Christ in His members.

There is also the power of politics. Of this the early Christians had no control; they had no influence whatever in the State. But this power is now in the hands of all. The work of a Wilberforce or a Shaftesbury shows what use can be made of it in putting an end to wrong and misery. It enables us to ascend the stream and cut great evils off at their sources. Christian men are only learning how to use it yet; some are even shy of touching it, as if it were unholy. But they will yet prize it as one of the most powerful instruments put by Providence into their hands for doing good. We shall not always be content with a philanthropy that picks up the victims as they fly broken from the wheel of oppression; we will stop the wheel itself.*

---

* "The obligation of philanthropy is for all ages, but if we consider the particular modes of philanthropy which Christ prescribed to His followers, we shall

These are only specimens of the powers with which Christian philanthropy is arming itself; and the strange word of Christ is coming true, "Verily, verily, I say unto you, he that believeth on Me, the works that I do shall he do also; and greater works shall he do, because I go unto My Father."

IV.

There is nothing more certain than that our Lord left this part of His work as an example to His followers. In the distribution of alms from the common bag He associated the Twelve with Himself, giving the bag in charge to one of them. To one who wished to join the company of those who followed Him He said, "Go and sell all that thou hast and give to the poor, and thou shalt have treasure in heaven, and come and follow Me;" and in other cases He may have imposed the same condition of discipleship. He associated the Twelve with Himself in like manner in the work of healing. "Heal the sick," He said, as He sent them forth,

---

find that they were suggested by the special conditions of that age. The same spirit of love which dictated them, working in this age upon the same problems, would find them utterly insufficient. No man who loves his kind can in these days rest content with waiting as a servant upon human misery, when it is in so many cases possible to anticipate and avert it. Prevention is better than cure, and it is now clear to all that a large part of human suffering is preventible by improved social arrangements. Charity will now, if it be genuine, fix upon this enterprise as greater, more widely and permanently beneficial, and therefore more Christian than the other. It will not, indeed, neglect the lower task of relieving and consoling those who, whether through the errors and unskilful arrangements of society or through causes not yet preventible, have actually fallen into calamity. . . . But when it has done all which the New Testament enjoins, it will feel that its task is not half fulfilled. When the sick man has been visited and everything done which skill and assiduity can do to cure him, modern charity will go on to consider the causes of his malady, what noxious influence besetting his life, what contempt of the laws of health in his diet or habits, may have caused it, and then to inquire whether others incur the same dangers and may be warned in time. When the starving man has been relieved, modern charity inquires whether any fault in the social system deprived him of his share of nature's bounty, any unjust advantage taken by the strong over the weak, any rudeness or want of culture in himself wrecking his virtue and his habits of thrift."—*Ecce Homo.*

"cleanse the lepers, raise the dead, cast out devils: freely ye have received, freely give."

But the most impressive evidence of all is His great description of the last judgment, where the King says to those on His right hand, "Come, ye blessed of My Father, inherit the kingdom prepared for you from the foundation of the world: for I was an hungered, and ye gave Me meat; I was thirsty, and ye gave Me drink; I was a stranger, and ye took Me in; naked, and ye clothed Me; I was sick, and ye visited Me; I was in prison, and ye came unto Me;" but to those on His left hand, "Depart from Me, ye cursed, into everlasting fire, prepared for the devil and his angels: for I was an hungered, and ye gave Me no meat; I was thirsty, and ye gave Me no drink; I was a stranger, and ye took Me not in; naked, and ye clothed Me not; sick, and in prison, and ye visited Me not."

Are there many Christians who realise that this is the test by which at the final review their Christianity is to be tried? Do the habits of Christendom accord with our Lord's plainest teaching? There are, indeed, a few who follow Him along this path. And, though it is a path of self-denial, they find it one of flowers; for on the way to the homes of the destitute they see the marks of His footsteps, and, in handling the bodies of the bedridden and suffering, their fingers touch His hands and His side. Thus, while losing their life, they find it. But is this a practice of the average Christian? Do his feet know the way to the homes of the blind, the tortured and the friendless? There is a day coming when many of us shall wish that every penny we have given to the poor had been a pound; when those who have begged from us on behalf of the suffering and the ignorant, but of whose importunities we have often complained, will be accounted our best benefactors; and when it will be more valuable to us to remember one hour passed in the garret of the poor than a hundred spent at the tables of the rich. "Inasmuch as ye have done it unto one of the least of these My brethren, ye have done it unto Me."

XII.

Christ as a Winner of Souls

Matt.   i. 21.
         iv. 18-22.
         ix. 10-13.

Luke   iv. 43.
         vii. 36-50.
         xv.
         xix. 1-10; 41, 42.
         xxii. 39-43.

John   ii. 23.
         iii.
         iv.
         vii. 31, 37.
         ix. 35-38.
         x. 11.
         xii. 21, 22.

CHAPTER XII.

Christ as a Winner of Souls.

I.

I have heard that one of the diamond-fields of South Africa was discovered on this wise. A traveller one day entered the valley and drew near to a settler's door, at which a boy was amusing himself by throwing stones. One of the stones fell at the stranger's feet, who picked it up and was in the act of laughingly returning it, when something flashed from it which stopped his hand and made his heart beat fast. It was a diamond. The child was playing with it as a common stone; the peasant's foot had spurned it; the cart-wheel had crushed it; till the man who knew saw it and recognised its value.

This story comes often to my mind when I am thinking of the soul. Was it not the same careless treatment the soul was receiving when Jesus arrived in the world and discovered it? A harlot's soul, sunk in the mud and filth of iniquity! why a Pharisee would not stain his fingers to find it. A child's soul! the scribes used to discuss in their schools whether or not a child had a soul at all.

Even yet there is nothing else of less account in the eyes of the majority than the soul. It is flung about, it is ignored, it is crushed by the careless foot, just as the undiscovered diamond was. A new soul, fresh out of eternity, enters an earthly home; but in most cases the family sin on as if it were not there; they are visited by no compunctions lest it should be corrupted by their example. By-and-bye it goes out into the world and is brought into contact with the multifarious influences of social life; but here there is, if possible, still less sense of its value; there is no fear of misleading it, no reverence for its high origin or its solemn destiny. If it remains undeveloped, or if it is lost and rushes unprepared upon its doom, the majority heed not; its fate is no business of theirs, and they do not even remember that it exists.

Our common language betrays that to the majority the soul is as undiscovered as the diamond was to the settler and his children. When the *employés* are pouring out of a factory at the meal hour, we say, What a number of hands! Hands! not souls; as if the body and the power of work in it were the whole of the man. Even the Church speaks of the population of the East End as the masses; as if they only counted in the bulk, and were not separable into units, in each of which there is that which touches heaven above and hell beneath. As we watch the multitude pouring along a crowded street, what is it we see? Only so many figures interesting or uninteresting for their looks, their dress and the like; or embodied spirits, that have come from God and are going to God?

If we have the power of seeing the latter, we have learned it from Christ. He lifted the soul up out of the mud and from among the trampling feet, and said, Behold the diamond! "What shall it profit a man if he gain the whole world and lose his own soul?"

Mankind believed, indeed, in the souls of the great—the soul that could distinguish itself by force or wisdom—the soul of Socrates, the soul of Caesar.* But Jesus taught it to believe in the common soul—the soul of a child, of a woman, nay, of a publican or a sinner. This is His immortal discovery. In every child of Adam He perceived the diamond. The rags of the beggar could

---

* "Contempt of men is a ground-feature of heathenism, which goes side by side with the deification of men, and we can trace this twofold extreme down to the heathenism of our own days."—MARTENSEN, *Christian Ethics.*

not hide it from His eyes, nor the black skin of the savage, nor even the crimes of the evil-doer. It was true the soul was lost sunk deep in ignorance and unrighteousness. But this only made it the more interesting; it only stimulated His desire to rescue and cleanse it, and set it where it might shine. To a physician who are interesting? Not they that are whole, but they who are sick; and among all his patients the most absorbing case is that which most needs his help. It haunts him day and night; it runs away with nine-tenths of his thinking; he visits it thrice a day; and, if the disease is overcome, this case is the triumph of his art. So Jesus taught, explaining His own feelings and conduct.

Yet there is a mystery in this estimate of the soul. Is it really true that one soul—that of the thief lying today in prison or of harlequin who was grinning last night in the circus—is more precious than the gold of California or the diamonds of Golconda? To multitudes, if they would confess the truth, such an assertion has no meaning. Yet it was made by Him who, while living here below in time, lived also aloft in eternity and could look clearly along the track of the future, seeing all that the soul can become—both the splendid possibilities it may develop and the depths to which it may fall.

This unique estimate of the soul was the secret spring of His work as a soul-winner; and it is this faith, kindling mind and heart, which makes the soul-winner always. A man has no claim to this office under any of its forms if he does not believe in the soul more than in money, or physique, or success, or any earthly thing, and unless the saving of a single soul would be to him a greater prize than all Greek and Roman fame.*

---

* "There is one power which lies at the bottom of all success in preaching; its influence is essential everywhere; without its presence we cannot imagine a man as making a minister of the Gospel in the largest sense. Under its compulsion a man becomes a preacher, and every sermon he preaches is more or less shaped by its presence. That power is the value of the human soul felt by the preacher, furnishing the motive and inspiration of all his work. . . . The other motives for the minister's work seem to me to stand around this great central motive as the staff-officers stand about the general. They need him, they execute

II.

There is another motive perhaps even more essential. It is the sense of a divine call. The soul-winner must be conscious that he is doing God's work, and that it is God's message he bears to men.

Enthusiasm for humanity is a noble passion and sheds a beautiful glow over the first efforts of an unselfish life. But it is hardly stern enough for the uses of the world. There come hours of despair when men seem hardly worth our devotion. They are so base and ungrateful, and our best efforts are able to change them so little, that the temptation is strong to throw up the thankless task. Those for whom we are sacrificing ourselves take all we can do as a matter of course; they pass us by unnoticed, or turn and rend us, as if we were their enemies. Why should we continue to press our gifts on those who do not want them? Worse still is the sickening consciousness that we have but little to give: perhaps we have mistaken our vocation; it is a world out of joint, but were we born to put it right? This is where a sterner motive is needed than love of men; our retreating zeal requires to be rallied by the command of God. It is His work; these souls are His; He has committed them to our care; and at the judgment-seat He will demand an account of them.

All prophets and apostles who have dealt with men for God have been driven on by this impulse, which has recovered them in hours of weakness and enabled them to face the opposition of the world. Most of them have experienced a crisis in which this

---

his will; but he is not dependent on them as they are on him. Any one of them might fall away, and he could fight the battle out without him. . . . Pleasure of work; delight in the exercise of power; love of God's truth; the love of study; gratification in feeling our life touch other lives; the perception of order; love of regular movement; insight into the lives and ways of men; and, lastly, the pleasure of seeing right ideas replace wrong ideas—these are the noble members of the staff of the great general. But how the motive which they serve towers above them all!" From a noble lecture on the value of the soul, with which Dr. Phillips Brooks closes his *Yale Lectures on Preaching*. The *locus classicus*, however, on this subject is Baxter's *Reformed Pastor*, through which the thought of the danger and the preciousness of the soul sounds like the bell of eternity.

call has come and clearly determined their life-work. It came to Moses in the wilderness and drove him into public life in spite of strong resistance; and it bore him through the unparalleled trials of his subsequent career. It came to Isaiah in a vision which coloured all his after history; and it revolutionised St. Paul's life in an hour. Jeremiah felt the divine message like a sword in his bones and like a fire which consumed him till he cast it forth among the people.*

This was one of the strongest motives of Christ's life also. It gave to it its irresistible momentum; it strengthened Him in the face of opposition; it rescued Him from the dark hour of despair. He was never weary of asserting that the works He did were not His own, but God's; and that so were the words He spoke. His comfort was that every step He took was in fulfilment of the divine will.

But He had no hour at which His life was broken in twain by a moral crisis, and the task of living for others imposed on Him. This vocation was inwoven with the very texture of His being; the love of men was as native to His heart as it is to the nature of God; the salvation of men was the primary passion of His soul; and, though He claimed that His works and words were given Him by God, yet so identified were His own deepest wishes with the purposes of the divine love, that He could say, "I and My Father are one."

III.

The name of Soul-winner which I have ventured to apply to the Saviour is a Scriptural one; for we read in Scripture that "he that winneth souls is wise." It is a word which indicates the delicacy and the difficulty of the work of seeking the lost. This work requires tact and skill in him who undertakes it. Souls have to be

---

* The difficult question of what constitutes a call to the ministry is discussed with great good sense in Blaikie's *For the Work of the Ministry*, and with racy wisdom in Spurgeon's *Lectures to My Students*.

won; and this requires a winning way—a kind of winsomeness—in those who seek them.

Jesus Himself did not use this word; but He made use of one suggestive of the same truth. When calling His disciples to take part with Him in this work, He said to them, "Follow Me, and I will make you fishers of men." Every fisher with the rod knows how much knowledge of the weather and the water, how much judgment, keenness of eye and lightness of touch fishing requires. Probably it was of net-fishing Christ was thinking; but this requires no less experience, alertness, tact and perseverance.

All these qualities are needed in winning souls. Jesus was the perfect model of this art; and the best guide to its acquisition is to watch His methods.

1. He made use of His miracles as stepping-stones to reach the soul. All the acts of kindness and mercy described in the foregoing chapter were introductions to the development of the higher and more spiritual aims which were always in His mind. I do not say that this was their only purpose; for His miracles had many meanings. But it was one of them: they often opened the door to spiritual dealing which could not have taken place without them. For example, in the ninth of St. John we read of a man whom He cured of blindness, without making Himself known to him. The man conceived a passion of gratitude and went about praising and championing his unknown friend; till Jesus, meeting him, made Himself known, when the man at once exclaimed, "Lord, I believe," and worshipped Him. This is a clear case in which the bodily cure was a prelude to the cure of the blindness of the soul. In numberless other instances it must have served the same end; and, if it be remembered that the miracles were often nearly as valuable to the relatives of those who were healed as to themselves, it will be understood how many minds must have been conciliated by this means to a favourable hearing of His divine message.

Philanthropy may serve us also as a stepping-stone to higher work. Kindness opens hearts; and through the open door salvation may be introduced. There lurks danger, indeed, on either hand; for, on the one hand, charity may be robbed of all true human kindliness by the proselytizer's zeal, and, on the other, a hypocritical pretence of piety may be put on by the receiver of temporal advantages, as a payment for the accepted dole. But, whilst these dangers need to be avoided, the principle itself has the highest authority, and in earnest Christian work it is receiving at present many happy applications. Zeal for the soul often awakens consideration for the body also, and produces deeds which smell as sweetly to the Saviour of men as did the ointment with which Mary anointed Him.

2. Preaching was one of the principal means by which Christ sought the lost. As a separate chapter occurs below on Jesus as a Preacher, the subject need not here be dwelt upon. Only let it be noted how attractive His preaching was—how well fitted to win men. He invested the truth with every charm of parable and illustration, though He well knew that such gay clothing is not truth's native garb. Truth is plain and simple; and those who know it love to have it so. But Jesus had to deal with those to whom in itself it had no attraction; and therefore He administered it to them as they were able to bear it, trusting that, if once it had won them and they had learned its worth, they would welcome it in any garb.

So powerful a means of winning men to God is preaching still, that it is no wonder that the desire to preach is often born at the same time as the desire of saving souls; but perhaps it is a wonder that of those who preach so few exert themselves, as Jesus did, to attract men by presenting their message in beautiful and winsome forms.*

---

* "Man irrt sich erstaunlich, wenn man meint, dass, was gerade so klingt, wie das Volk in den Arbeitsstunden selbst redet, von diesem am liebsten gehört werde. Sie haben den Sonntagsrock angezogen, als sie in die Kirche gegangen sind; so thut es ihnen auch wohl, an der Predigt, die sie vernehmen, das festliche Kleid zu gewahren." From the Preface to Tholuck's *Predigten*, where will be found some of the most remarkable pages on Preaching ever written.

3. Of course only a small proportion of those who burn to save the lost can become preachers; but with His preaching Jesus combined another method, which it is more open to all to imitate—the method of conversation. We have illustrations of His use of this method in His conversation with Nicodemus and His talk at the well with the woman of Samaria, which are models, intended to serve to all time, of this mode of winning souls. If the two cases be compared together, it will be seen with what perfect tact He adapted Himself to the circumstances of His interlocutors, and how naturally, whilst meeting them on their own ground, He led the conversation to the point He aimed at, always descending full upon the conscience.

This is a difficult art; for religious conversation must be natural—it must well up out of a heart full of religion—or it is worse than useless. Yet it is of priceless value, and no trouble is too great to be spent in acquiring it. I am not sure but we are more in need of those who can talk about religion than of those who can preach about it. A sermon is often applied by the hearers to one another, whilst each puts its message away from himself; but conversation goes straight to its mark. If it is supported by an impressive and consistent character, he who can wield it carries a blessing with him wherever he goes; in homes in which he has been a visitor his memory is cherished as that of one who has made religion real; and, though his name may be little heard of on earth, his track through the world is marked by a line of light to the eye of Heaven.

Jesus did not, however, need always to be the aggressor when employing this instrument. In many cases those whom He conversed with about the concerns of the soul introduced the subject themselves. Persons who were anxious about religion sought Him out; for they instinctively felt that He knew the way after which they were groping. The passing of Jesus through the country was like the passing of a magnet over a floor where there are pieces of iron: it drew the souls which had affinity for the divine life to itself. And in all Christian communities there are some who, in greater or less degree, discharge the same function. They are known to possess the secret of life; those passing through the deepest experiences of the soul are confident that they will understand them; burdened consciences seek their sympathy. Surely this is the most precious privilege of the soul-winner: he is never so effectively seeking the lost as when the lost seek him.

IV.

As our subject in these chapters is the imitation of Christ, we naturally dwell on those aspects of His life and work in which it is possible for us to imitate Him. But ever and anon we need to remember at what a height He is above us. It is only with distant and faltering steps we can follow Him at all; and in many places He passes quite beyond our reach.

It is so at this point. In some respects, such as those just mentioned, we can imitate Him in winning souls; but He went, in this quest, where we cannot go: He came not only to seek but to save the lost. He compared Himself, as a soul-winner, to the shepherd going after the lost sheep and bringing it home on his shoulders rejoicing; and thus far we may venture to compare our own soul-winning to His; but He carried the comparison further "The good shepherd giveth his life for the sheep." He followed sinners to their earthly haunts, and so may we; but He followed them further—down to the gates of hell, where He plucked the prey from the hands of the mighty. He entered a supernatural region, where He conquered for us, made atonement for us, opened for us the gates of immortality. Of these transactions we can but dimly know, for they were done in a region which we have not seen. Only we know that they were greater—more pathetic and solemn—than all our thoughts. The outward sign and symbol of them which we can see is Golgotha—His body broken for us, His blood shed for us. And this is the highest symbol of soul-winning love.

Here we rather bow down and adore than think of imitation. Yet here too there are lessons which all must learn who wish to be expert in this art. No one will have power with men who has not power with God for men; the victory may seem to be won whilst we persuade men, but it has to be previously won in the place of intercession. This place was to Jesus a place of agony and death; and there is no soul-winning without pain and sacrifice. St. Paul said that he filled up that which was lacking in the sufferings of Christ for His body's sake, which is the Church; and all who will be partakers of Christ's joy in the redemption of the world must first be partakers in His sufferings.

V.

If the art of the soul-winner is difficult and accompanied with much pain, its reward is correspondingly great. I have known an eminent portrait-painter, who, when the crisis of his picture came at which it was to be determined whether or not he had produced a likeness of the features only, or a picture of the soul and character of his subject, used to fall into perfect paroxysms of excitement, weeping, wringing his hands and grovelling on the ground; but, when it was over and the true likeness stood embodied on the canvas, gave way to equally extravagant exultation. And it must be a strange sensation to see an image of beauty, out of nothing so to speak, gradually developing itself on the canvas and living there. But what is this compared with seeing a soul emerging from death into life—its wings freeing themselves from the hard, ugly chrysalis of its natural condition, to flutter forth into the sunshine of eternity?

Of the effect of this sight on Jesus we have an authentic glimpse in the wonderful parables of the fifteenth of St. Luke— the shepherd calling his friends together and saying, "Rejoice with me, for I have found my sheep which was lost," and the father of the prodigal crying, "Let us eat and drink and be merry." He has told us Himself what this rejoicing means: "Verily I say unto you, There is joy in the presence of the angels of God over one sinner that repenteth." And that joy in the faces of the angels is only a reflection of the joy of the Lord of angels, on whose face they are ever gazing.

In His earthly life we see very clearly on at least one occasion this holy excitement in His heart.* When He had won the wicked woman of Samaria to God and holiness, His disciples, arriving where He was with provisions which they brought from the town, prayed Him, saying, "Master, eat." But He could not eat; He was too delighted and absorbed; and He answered, "I have meat to eat that ye know not of." Then, looking towards the city, whither the woman had gone to bring more souls to Him to be won, He continued in the same enraptured strain, "Say not ye, There are yet four months, and then cometh harvest? Behold, I say unto you, Lift up your eyes, and look on the fields; for they are white already to harvest." It was the same deep passion in another phase, when He beheld the city which He had in vain attempted to win and in which so many souls were perishing, and wept over it.

In these sacred emotions all soul-winners partake in their degree; and there are no higher emotions in this world. They are the signature and patent of a nobility derived directly from Heaven; for the humblest Christian worker, who is really pained with the sin of men and rejoices in their salvation, is feeling, in his degree, the very passion which bore the Saviour of the world through His sufferings, and which has throbbed from eternity in the heart of God.

---

* I have heard the late Brownlow North say that, though on one side of His nature Jesus was the Man of Sorrows, on another He was the happiest of all the children of men.

XIII.

Christ as a Preacher

Matt.	iv. 16; 23-25.
	v.-vii.
	ix. 4, 13; 35-38.
	x. 7, 19, 20; 27.
	xiii.
	xvi. 14.
Mark	i. 38, 39.
	ii. 2.
	iv. 33.
	vi. 1-6.
Luke	iv. 16-32.
	v. 17.
	vii. 16.
	viii. 1-8.
	xi. 27, 28.
John	iii. 34.
	vii. 14-16; 26; 40; 45, 46.
	viii. 1, 2.

CHAPTER XIII.

Christ as a Preacher.

I.

If, in the course of a lifetime, we have been fortunate enough to hear once or twice an orator of the first rank, we talk of it all our days; or, if we can remember a preacher who first made religion real to us, his image is enshrined in our memory in a sacred niche. What, then, must it have been to listen to Him who spake as never man spake? What must it have been to hear the Sermon on the Mount or the Parable of the Prodigal Son issuing, for the first time, fresh from the lips that uttered them?

For thirty years Jesus had kept silence. During this period the waters of thought and conviction had been accumulating in His mind; and, when the outlet was opened, forth they rushed in copious volume. He began in Nazareth and Capernaum, the places of His abode, to preach in the synagogues on the Sabbaths. But He soon extended His activity to the neighbouring villages and towns. Nor were the Sabbaths and the synagogues and the customary hours of worship sufficient for His zeal; by-and-bye He was preaching every day, and not only in the synagogues, but in streets and squares, and in the more picturesque temple of the hillside or the seashore.

The enthusiasm of those whom He addressed corresponded with His own. Almost as soon as He began to preach His fame spread over the whole of Syria, bringing hearers from every quarter; and from this time onwards we are constantly hearing that great multitudes followed Him, the crowd becoming sometimes so dense that they trode one upon another. They detained Him when, wearied out with His efforts, He wished to escape into solitude; and, if at length He got away for a little, they were waiting for Him when He came back.

All classes were to be found in His audiences. Not unfrequently the preacher who can move the populace is neglected by the educated, whilst he who can satisfy the cultured few is caviare to the general. But at the feet of Jesus you might have seen Pharisees and doctors of the law sitting, who were come out of every town of Galilee and Judæa and Jerusalem; whilst, on the other hand, the common people heard Him gladly; and even the class below the line of respectability—those who in general cared nothing for synagogues and sermons—were roused for once to frequent the public religious assemblies: "Then drew near unto Him all the publicans and sinners for to hear Him."

Wherein lay the secret of this intense and universal interest? The ancients represented the orator in works of art as drawing men after himself with golden chains issuing from his mouth. What were the chains of attraction by which Jesus drew all men unto Himself?

II.

When the standard of religious life and of preaching is conspicuously low in a country or neighbourhood, the appearance of a man of God who preaches the Word with power is made remarkable by contrast; the darkness of the background making the light more visible.

A darkness of this kind, which may be compared to that of midnight, was brooding over Galilee when Jesus opened His career as a preacher; and St. Matthew, who lived on the spot, describes the contrast by quoting these words of prophecy: "The people that sat in darkness saw great light; and to them who sat in the region and shadow of death light is sprung up." In the same way, the first criticism passed on the new Preacher by all who heard Him was a surprised expression of the difference they felt between Him and their accustomed teachers: "The people were astonished at His doctrine; for He taught them as one having authority, and not as the scribes."

The scribes were their accustomed teachers, who harangued them week by week in the synagogues. No doubt there must have been differences among them; they cannot all have been equally bad; but, taken as a whole, they were probably the most barren and unspiritual set of men who have ever held sway over the mind of a nation. In the collection of Jewish books called the Talmud, which has come down to us and is, indeed, at present in process of being translated into the English language, we have specimens of their teaching, and those who have studied them declare that they are the driest products of the human mind. To read them is like travelling through endless galleries of lumber, where the air is darkened and the lungs are well-nigh asphyxiated with the rising dust.

The people in their criticism of Jesus exactly hit the principal defect of their teachers. He, they said, taught with authority, and not as the scribes; that is, the scribes taught without authority. This is the leading characteristic of these Talmudic writings. No teacher speaks as if he had ever been in touch with God Himself or seen the spiritual world with his own eyes. Everyone quotes some earlier teacher, to whose authority he appeals; they are all leaning upon one another. This is a fatal kind of preaching, though it has often prevailed and sometimes loudly arrogated to itself the name of orthodoxy. Have you never heard God spoken of as if He had existed hundreds of years ago, in Bible times, but no longer moved and worked in the life and history of today? Have you never heard joy in God, the happiness of forgiveness, the fulness of the Spirit, and the other higher experiences of the spiritual life, spoken of as if they had, indeed, been experienced by the saints of the Bible, but were no longer to be looked for in these modern centuries? The Bible can be converted into a prison in which God is confined, or a museum in which the spiritual life is preserved as an antiquarian curiosity. But those who came to hear Jesus felt that He was in direct contact with the spiritual world and brought to them news of what He had Himself seen and felt. He was not a mere commentator, repeating some faint and far-derived echo of the message received from on high by men long dead. He spoke like one who had just come from the abode of the Highest, or rather who was still in it, seeing what He was describing. He was not a scribe, but a prophet, who could say, "Thus saith the Lord."

So the fame of Him travelled from Dan to Beersheba; men said to one another, with kindling looks, "A great prophet is risen up among us;" and the shepherd left his sheep in the wilderness, the husbandman his vineyard, and the fisher his nets by the shore, to go and hear the new Preacher; for men know they need a message from the other world, and they instinctively recognise the authentic voice when they hear it.

III.

Preaching sometimes acquires an extraordinary influence from the personality of the preacher. Those who have merely read the sermon are told by those who have heard it that they have no conception of what it was: "You should have seen the man." It is well known that the posthumously published discourses of some of the greatest pulpit orators have entirely disappointed the world, posterity asking in surprise where the influence can have lain. It lay in the man—in the peculiarity of his personality—in the majesty of his appearance, or his passionate earnestness, or his moral force.

It cannot be said that the printed words of Jesus are disappointing: on the contrary, their weightiness and originality must have attracted attention however they had been spoken. But yet in this case, also, as can easily be perceived from the criticism of His hearers, the Preacher told as well as the sermon.

We do not, indeed, know how Jesus looked—whether His appearance was attractive, His voice pleasant, or the like; the traditions about such things which have come down to us not being trustworthy. But we do know in some respects the nature of the impressions which He made on His hearers.

Though for many generations the only preachers whom His countrymen had heard were dry-as-dust scribes, yet one of the proudest traditions of the Jewish people was the memory of great speakers for God whose voices had sounded throughout the land in days gone by, and whose characteristics were indelibly imprinted on the national memory; and, as soon as Jesus commenced to preach, it was recognised at once that the great order of the Prophets had revived in Him. They said He spoke as one of the prophets.

But they went further: they actually believed that one or other of the old prophets had risen from the dead and resumed his work in the person of Jesus. In indulging this fancy, they were divided between two of the ancient prophets, and the selection of these two clearly shows what characteristics they had specially remarked in Him. The two were Jeremiah and Elijah: some said He was Jeremiah, others that He was Elijah.

Now these were both great prophets; perhaps the very greatest in the popular estimation; so that it was to their very greatest that they compared Him. But the two were of types so diametrically opposite to one another that it may seem impossible that their characteristics should have been united in one personality.

Jeremiah was the soft, pathetic prophet—the man of heart, who wished that his eyes were a fountain of tears to weep for the misfortunes of his people. It is not surprising that Christ's hearers discovered a resemblance to him; for it must have been evident at the first glance that Jesus was a man of heart. The very first sentences of His Sermon on the Mount were words of compassion for the poor, the mourners, the oppressed. The most insignificant among His hearers must have felt that He took an interest in him and would take any trouble to do him good. Although He addressed all classes, His boast was that He preached the Gospel to the poor; whilst the scribes flattered the wealthy and coveted cultivated audiences, the common man knew that Jesus considered his soul as precious as that of the wealthiest of His hearers. The sight of a multitude moved Him with a strange compassion. And, like Jeremiah, He was such an intense lover of His country and His countrymen, that even the publican or harlot was dear to Him because belonging to the seed of Abraham.

Elijah was in every respect a contrast to Jeremiah: he was a man of rock, who could rebuke kings and queens to their faces and stand alone against the world. It did not seem possible that one who exhibited the traits of Jeremiah should also exhibit those of Elijah. Yet the people recognised in Jesus an Elijah. And they were not mistaken. It is an entire misapprehension to suppose that Jesus was all softness and gentleness. There was a sternness in many of His utterances not surpassed even by Elijah's rebukes of Ahab, and the bold denunciation of wrong was one of the most imposing elements of His power. There has never been in this world a polemic so uncompromising and annihilating as His against the Pharisees.

The truth is, both characteristics, His softness and His sternness, had a common root. As in the poorest peasant He saw and revered a man, so in the wealthiest noble He saw no more than a man. As the rags of Lazarus could not conceal from Him the dignity of the soul, so the purple of Dives could not blind Him to its meanness. He knew what was in man—the height and the depths, the glory and the shame, the pathos and the horror; and men felt, as they faced Him, that here was One whose manhood towered above their own and yet, stooping down, embraced it and sympathized with it through and through.

IV.

No preacher has perhaps ever made a profound impression on the general mind who has not studied the form in which to put what he has had to say; or perhaps the fact might be more correctly stated by saying, that the true messenger from God to the people instinctively clothes his message in attractive and arresting words. Beginners in preaching, I observe, are apt to neglect this: they think that, if only they have something good to say, it does not matter how they say it. As well might a housewife suppose that, if only she has something good to give her guests to eat, it does not matter how it is cooked.

The teaching of Jesus owed its attractiveness, and owes it still, in no small degree, to its exquisite form. The common people do not, I think, as a rule remember so well the drift of an argument or a long discourse as remarks here and there expressed in pithy, pointed, crystalline words. This is the form of most of the sayings of Jesus. They are simple, felicitous and easily remembered; yet every one of them is packed full of thought, and the longer you brood over it the more do you see in it. It is like a pool so clear and sunny that it seems quite shallow, till, thrusting in your stick to touch the pebbles so clearly visible at the bottom, you discover that its depth far exceeds what you are trying to measure it with.

But the discourses of Jesus had a still more popular quality: they were plentifully adorned with illustrations. This is the most attractive quality of human speech. The same God being the Author of both the world of mind and the world of matter, He has so fashioned them that the objects of nature, if presented in a certain way, become mirrors in which are reflected the truths of the spirit; and we are so constituted that we never relish truth so well as when it is presented in this way. Nature contains thousands of these mirrors for exhibiting spiritual truth which have never yet been used but await the hands of the masters of speech who are yet to be born.

Christ used this method of illustrating truth so constantly that the common objects of the country in which He resided are seen more perfectly in His words than in all the historians of the time. The Jewish life of Galilee in the days of Christ is thus lifted up out of the surrounding darkness into everlasting visibility, and, as on the screen of a magic lantern, we see, in scene after scene, the landscapes of the country, the domestic life of the people, and the larger life of the cities in all their details. In the house we see the cup and the platter, the lamp and the candlestick; we see the servants grinding the meal between the millstones and then hiding the leaven in it, till the whole is leavened; we see the mother of the family sewing a piece of cloth on an old garment and the father straining the wine into the skin-bottles; we see, at the door, the hen gathering her chickens under her wings and, in the streets, the children playing at marriages and funerals. Out in the fields we see the lilies in their stately beauty rivalling Solomon's, the crows picking up the seed behind the sower, and the birds in their nests among the branches; the doves and the sparrows, dogs and swine, the fig tree and the bramble bush. Looking up, we see the cloud carried over the landscape by the south wind, the red sky of evening promising fair weather for the morrow, and the lightning flashing from one end of heaven to the other. We see the vineyard with its tower and winepress; the field adorned with the tender blade of spring or sprinkled with the reapers among the yellow grain of autumn; the sheep, too, yonder on their pastures, and the shepherd going before them or seeking the lost one far over hill and dale. Are there any figures of our own streets with which we are more familiar than the Pharisee and the Publican at prayer in the Temple; or the Priest and the Levite and the Good Samaritan on the road to Jericho; or the gorgeous Dives at his daily banquet and Lazarus lying at his gate with the dogs licking his sores? Nor were these pictures less striking to the audiences of Jesus, though they were familiar; for—

> We're made so that we love
> First when we see them painted, things we've passed
> Perhaps a hundred times, nor cared to see.

It was because Jesus had exquisite love and consideration for His hearers that He thus sought out acceptable words to win their minds. But there was a reason in Himself besides. It is when the mind of a preacher is acting on the truth with intense energy and delight that it coruscates in such gleams of illustration. When the mental energy is only smouldering in a lukewarm way inside the subject, then you have the commonplace, prosaic statement; when the warmth increases and pervades the whole, you get the clear, strong, impressive statement; but, when the glow has thoroughly mastered the mass and flames all over it, then come the gorgeous images and parables which dwell for ever in the minds of the hearers.

V.

However important the form of preaching may be, the supremely momentous thing is the substance of it. The form is only the stamp of the coin; but the substance is the metal. What is that—is it gold or silver, or only copper? is it genuine or counterfeit? This is the all-important question.

Never has the substance of preaching been more trivial than among the Jewish scribes. The Talmudical books show this. The topics they deal with are in their triviality beneath contempt. The religion of the scribes was a mere round of ceremonies, and their preaching was almost wholly occupied with these: the proper breadth of phylacteries, the proper length of fasts, the articles on which tithe ought to be paid, the hundred and one things by which one might be made ceremonially unclean—these and a thousand similar minutiæ formed the themes of their tiresome harangues. There have been times in the history of the Church since then when the pulpit has sunk almost to as low a level. In our own country immediately before the Reformation the sermons of the monks were, if possible, even worse—more trivial and low in tone—than those of the scribes in the time of Christ. Similarly in Germany last century, when Rationalism was at its lowest, the pulpit had reached an almost incredible stage of degradation.* The truth is, there is a necessity in these things. When the minds

---

* "Die Zeit der Kaffee- und Kuhpocken-Predigten" it is wittily named by Tholuck, referring, I fancy, to the subjects of some notorious sermons.

of preachers grow cold, they move away insensibly from the central things and drift to those on the circumference; and at length they go over the circumference.

Of course the subjects which formed the substance of Christ's preaching cannot here be enumerated. It must suffice to say that His matter was always the most solemn and vital which can be presented to the human mind. He spoke of God in such a way that His hearers felt as if to their eyes God was now light and in Him was no darkness at all. As He uttered such parables as the Lost Sheep and the Prodigal Son, it seemed as if the gates of heaven were thrown open and they could see the very beatings of the heart of the divine mercy. He spoke of man so as to make every hearer feel that till that moment he had never been acquainted either with himself or with the human race. He made every man conscious that he carried in his own bosom that which was more precious than worlds; and that the passing hours of his apparently trivial life were charged with issues reaching high as heaven and deep as hell. When He spoke of eternity, He brought life and immortality, which men before then had only vaguely guessed at, fully to light, and described the world behind the veil with the graphic and familiar force of one to whom it was no unknown country.

Is it any wonder that the crowds followed Him, that they hung spellbound on His lips and could never get enough of His preaching? Intoxicated as men are with the secularities of this world, they know, deep down, that they belong to another, and, interesting as the knowledge of this world is, the questions about the other world will always be far more fascinating to the spirit of man. Whence am I? What am I? Whither am I going? Unless preaching can answer these questions, we may shut our churches. That voice which sounded on the Galilean mountain-side, and which spoke of these mysteries so familiarly, we, indeed, shall never hear, till we hear it from the great white throne. But the heart and the spirit that embodied themselves in these sounds never die; they live and burn to-day as they did then. Whenever a preacher strikes correctly a note of the eternal truth, it is Christ that does it. Whenever a preacher makes you feel that there is a world of realities above and behind the one you see and touch; whenever he lays hold of your mind, touches your heart, awakens your aspiration, rouses your conscience—that is Christ trying to grasp you, to reach you with His love, to save you. "Now then we are ambassadors for Christ; as though God did beseech you by us, we pray you in Christ's stead, be ye reconciled to God."

XIV.

Christ as a Teacher

Matt.   iv. 18, 19.
ix. 9; 14-17.
x.
xii. 1-3; 49.
xiii. 10, 11; 16-36.
xv. 15, 16; 23, 24; 32; 36.
xvi. 5-28.
xvii.
xviii. 1-3; 21, 22.
xix. 13-30.
xx. 17-19; 20-28.
xxvi. 21, 22; 26-36; 56.
xxviii. 7, 10, 16-20.

Mark   iii. 1.
iv. 34.
vi. 30-32.
ix. 35-41.
xvi. 7.

Luke   ix. 54-56.
x. 1-17.
xi. 1.
xxiv. 36-51.

John   ii. 11, 22.
iv. 2.
xiii.-xvii.

CHAPTER XIV.

Christ as a Teacher.

I.

The function of the teacher is a more limited one than that of the preacher. The preacher addresses the multitude; the teacher concentrates his attention on a select few. The audiences to whom Jesus preached numbered thousands; the men to whom He acted as teacher numbered only twelve. Yet perhaps in its results His work in the latter capacity was quite equal in value to His whole work as a preacher.

The teacher's office had many remarkable occupants before Christ. In the schools of Greek philosophy Socrates, Plato, Aristotle and other famous masters stood in a relation to their disciples similar to that which Jesus sustained to His. Among the Jews also this relationship was not unknown. In the schools of the prophets, in the Old Testament, the "men of God" were the teachers of "the sons of the prophets." John the Baptist, besides preaching to the multitude, had disciples who followed him.

The standing phrase in Greek for the disciples of any master is "those about him:" the disciples of Socrates, for example, are "those about Socrates." Similarly it is said in the Gospels that Jesus chose the Twelve "that they should be with Him." This circumstance alone must have limited the number of those who were His disciples in the strict sense; for few could give up their work and home in order to follow Him. His habits were itinerant; and this made the separation of those about Him from settled occupations more absolute. It seems, indeed, that some attached themselves to Him temporarily and intermittently; for we hear on one occasion of as many as a hundred and twenty disciples, and on another of seventy; but those whom He chose out to give up all and be with Him continually were only twelve.

There was, however, another reason for the strict limitation of their number. A teacher has to know his disciples individually and study them, as a mother has to study the temperament of each of her children separately in order to be to them a good mother. While the preacher, addressing a crowd, draws the bow at a venture, not knowing whom he may hit, and has carefully to avoid references to particular persons, the teacher addresses every question and remark straight to individuals; and therefore he must know the precise mental condition of every one before him. This is why the names of the Twelve are so exactly given in evangelist after evangelist, and their relations to one another indicated. Perhaps they included as great a variety of disposition and experience as will ever be found among the same number of men; but they were not too numerous for separate treatment, and there is the completest evidence that their Master studied every one of them till He knew him through and through, and carefully adapted His treatment to each particular case. His affectionate way with John exactly suited the temperament of that disciple; and equally adapted to the case was His patient and delicate handling of Thomas. But His treatment of Peter was the crown and glory of His activity in this character. How completely He knew him! He managed the tumultuous and fluctuating elements of his character as a perfect rider does a high-mettled horse. And how successful He was! He transformed a nature unstable as water into the consistency of rock; and on this rock He built the Church of the New Testament. Similar results were achieved in the whole apostolic circle. With the exception of the traitor, every one of the

Twelve became, by means of the Master's teaching, able to be a pillar in the Church and a power in the world.

Jesus combined the work of the preacher and that of the teacher. The former was most fascinating, and it could easily have absorbed His whole time and strength. The multitudes were clamorous to have Him, and their needs spoke urgently to His heart. Yet He saved most of His time for the training of twelve men. We love numbers too much. We measure ministerial success by them; and many servants of God expend on them their whole strength. It is true, indeed, that no preacher who has the heart of Jesus in his breast can join in the depreciation of the multitude which sounds so wise, but is so cheap. Yet the example of Jesus teaches us also a different lesson. It is a saying of one of the wise, that the difference between being broad and being narrow is the difference between being a marsh and being a stream; and the quaint remark has a bearing on the present case. If a moderate quantity of force, such as may be in us, is distributed over too wide a surface, it may have no more effect than the inch-deep water of a marsh; but, concentrated on a more limited task, it may be like a stream which sings along its narrow channel and drives the mill. Get a multitude and distribute your influence over it, and every one may receive but little; but throw yourself on twelve men or six or even one, and the effects may be deep and everlasting. There are those quite unfit to address a multitude who might teach a small number; and it may turn out in the end that they have done as much as if they had been endowed with the more coveted gift.

II.

In some respects Christ's methods of teaching the Twelve were similar to those which He pursued with the multitude. They heard all His addresses to the multitude, for they were always with Him; whereas the majority of His hearers can only have heard Him once or twice. Besides, they heard from Him in private many a discourse not dissimilar in its structure to His public sermons. In the same way, they witnessed all His miracles, because they accompanied Him wherever He went; whereas the majority saw only the miracles performed in one or two places. Besides, He wrought some of His very greatest miracles—such, for example, as the stilling of the tempest—in their presence and for their benefit alone. This constant repetition of great impressions was an incalculable advantage.

But that which was distinctive in His method of dealing with them was the permission He gave them to put questions, which He answered. Whenever there was anything in His public discourses which was obscure, they asked Him in private what it meant, and He told them. Or, if they had hesitation about the truth or wisdom of anything He stated, they were at liberty to propound their doubts, and He solved them. Thus, at the beginning of His ministry, we find them asking why He spake in parables, and again and again afterwards they requested Him to explain a parable which they had not fully understood. When they heard His severe teaching on divorce, they said to Him, "If the case of the man be so with his wife, it is not good to marry," and drew from Him a fuller statement on the subject. In the same way, when they heard Him say that it is easier for a camel to go through the eye of a needle than for a rich man to enter into the kingdom of God, they exclaimed, "Who then can be saved?" and thus led Him on to a copious discourse on the subject of riches. In short, we are told that, "when He was alone, He expounded all things to His disciples."

But He pursued this method further: He not only allowed them to ask questions, but provoked them to do so. He deliberately wound His statements in obscurity and paradox to excite the questioning propensity. He Himself gave this explanation of His habit of speaking in parables. The parable was a veil cast over the face of the truth for the very purpose of tempting the hearers to lift it and see the beauty which it half concealed and half revealed. A teacher has done nothing unless he awakens the mind to independent activity. As long as it is merely passive, receiving what is poured into it but doing nothing more, true education has not commenced. It is only when the mind itself begins to work on a subject, feeling within itself difficulties to which the truth supplies the answers, and wants to which it gives satisfaction, that growth commences and progress is made. What Christ said set the minds of His disciples in a ferment; it was intended to raise in them all sorts of perplexities, and then they came to Him for their solution.

The method of Socrates, the wisest of heathen teachers, was similar. In his teaching also questioning played a prominent part. When a disciple came to him, Socrates would ask a question on some important subject, such as righteousness, temperance or wisdom, about which the disciple believed himself to be perfectly well-informed. His answer would be replied to by another question, designed to make him doubt whether it was correct or sufficient. Then Socrates would go on asking question after question from twenty different sides and angles of the subject, till the disciple was made to see that his own opinions about it were, as yet, nothing but a confused bundle of contradictions, and probably also that his mind itself was a mass of undigested pulp.[*]

Both methods had the same end—to excite the mind to independent activity. Yet there is a subtle and profound distinction between them. Socrates asked questions which his disciples tried to answer; Jesus provoked His disciples to ask questions which He answered. On the whole, what was aimed at in the school of philosophy was the mental gymnastic; the answers to the questions did not matter so much. Indeed, many philosophers have avowed that the chief end of their work is the mental invigoration obtained in the pursuit of truth;[†] and the saying of one of them is well known, that, if the Deity were to offer him in one hand the

---

* Description by Dr. Chalmers of a foolish preacher; story still remembered in Kirkcaldy.

† Compare the witty remark of NOVALIS (*Schriften*, vol. iii., p. 196): "Der Philosoph lebt von Problemen wie der Mensch von Speisen. Ein unauflösliches Problem ist eine unverdauliche Speise. Was die Würze an den Speisen, das ist das Paradoxe an den Problemen. Wahrhaft aufgelöst wird ein Problem wenn es als solches vernichtet wird. So auch mit den Speisen. Der Gewinn von Beiden

pursuit of truth and in the other the truth itself, he would unhesitatingly choose the former. This may be a wise saying in the region of philosophy; but no wise man would make it in the region of religion. It was saving truth of which Jesus was a teacher. The pursuit of this also disciplines the mind, but we dare not be satisfied with the pursuit alone; we must have the answers to the great questions of the soul. Therefore, whilst Socrates questioned, Jesus answered; and to Him, after wandering in the obscurities of doubt and inquiry, men will always have at last to come for the solution of the problems of the spirit. "Lord, to whom shall we go? Thou hast the words of eternal life."

III.

If we were to express the aim of Christ in the training of the Twelve by saying that it was to provide successors to Himself, we should be using too strong a word; for of course in His greatest and most characteristic work—the working out of redemption by His sufferings and death—He had, and could have, no successor. He finished the work, leaving nothing for anyone else to do.

But, this being understood, we may perhaps best express what He did as a teacher by saying that He was training His own successors. When He was taken from the earth, much that He had been wont to do, and would have continued to do had He remained here, fell to them. They had to undertake the championing of the cause which He had founded, and its guidance in the world. From the very beginning of His own activity He had had this in view; and, in spite of preoccupations, which would, if He had allowed them, have entirely absorbed Him, He devoted Himself to the preparation of those who should take His place after His departure.

---

ist die Thätigkeit, die bei Beiden erregt wird. Jedoch gibt es auch nährende Probleme wie nährende Speisen, deren Elemente ein Zuwachs meiner Intelligenz werden."

He employed them at first in subordinate and ministerial branches of His own work. For example, it is expressly said that "Jesus baptized not, but His disciples." After they had been longer with Him and attained to some degree of Christian maturity, He sent them forth to labour on their own account. They made tours, perhaps of no great extent, preaching and healing, and then returned to tell Him "all things, both what they had done and what they had taught," and to receive instructions for further operations. In this way the ground was sometimes broken up by the disciples before the Master came to sow it with the seed of eternal life; and perhaps regions were overtaken which He had not time to visit in person. But above all, their powers were being developed and their faith strengthened in view of the day, which He foresaw, when they would find themselves left alone face to face with the task of founding the Church and conquering the world in His name.

It is one of the characteristics of genuine Christianity, that it gives us an interest not only in the great events of the past, but also in the history of the future. The average man cares little for the future, except so far perhaps as his own offspring may be concerned: if he is happy, what does it matter to him what the state of the world will be after he is dead? But to a Christian it does matter. The faith and love in his heart bind him to the saints yet unborn. He is interested in a cause which is to go on after he has left it, and which he is to meet and take up again at a subsequent stage of his existence. It is almost as important to him how the work of Christ will be prospering when he is in his grave as how it is prospering now. This ought to make us think anxiously of those who are to be doing our work after we have left it. Christ thought of this from the very commencement of His own activity; and it was not too soon.

A man may do more for a cause by bringing younger forces into its service and training them to their work than by lavishing on it every moment of his own time and every atom of his energy. I was recently reading a monograph on the history of a particular branch of medicine; and intensely interesting it was to trace the progress from the beginning of knowledge among the Greek naturalists down through the Arab physicians of the Middle Ages, till one came to the vast and daily multiplying discoveries of modern science. But the name in the whole succession which chiefly arrested my attention was that of one whose contributions had been very large, but who acknowledged that they had not been strictly his own. He was always surrounded by a group of young physicians whom he inspired with enthusiasm for his subject; then he was in the habit of giving them single points of obscurity to investigate; and it was by the accumulation of these detailed studies that he was able to make vast additions to science. We need nothing more pressingly in the Christian Church at present than men who will thus guide the young and the willing to their work, showing what needs to be done and adapting talent to task. By taking up this function of the teacher, many a man might bring into the service of Christ those whose contributions would far surpass his own, as Barnabas did, when he brought into the Church the services of Paul

IV.

Perhaps in our modern life the work most closely resembling the work of Jesus as a teacher is that of a professor of divinity.* The students in our theological seminaries and colleges are at the same stage as the Twelve were before they were sent forth on their independent course; and the intercourse between Christ and the Twelve, if carefully studied, would throw much light on the relationship between professors and students.

---

* In *The Public Ministry and Pastoral Methods of our Lord* Professor Blaikie heads a chapter, "The College of the Twelve." He also suggests another analogy: "A young minister, for example, may try to multiply himself by means of the young men of his flock. Some have a rare gift of finding out the most susceptible of these—getting them about them in classes and meetings, and perhaps sometimes in walks and at meals—explaining to them their plans, infusing into

To the Twelve the most valuable part of their connection with Christ was simply the privilege of being with Him—of seeing that marvellous life day by day, and daily receiving the silent, almost unobserved, impress of His character. St. John, reflecting on this three years' experience long afterwards, summed it up by saying, "We beheld His glory!" The word he uses denotes the shekinah that shone above the mercy-seat. In those lonely walks through Phœnicia and Peræa, in those close talks on the hills of Galilee, they often felt that the holy of holies was being opened to them, and that they were gazing on the beauty that is ineffable.

The chief defect perhaps of theological training, as it is practised at present, is the lack of this close intercourse between the teacher and the taught. Few professors have attempted it on any considerable scale. It would, indeed, be trying work. No eyes are so keen as those of students. If admitted close to a man, they take immediate stock of his resources. They are hero-worshippers when they believe in a professor; but their scorn is unmeasured if they disbelieve in him. They can be dazzled by a reputation; but only massiveness of character and thoroughness of attainment can be sure of permanently impressing them.

I know of only one man in recent times who threw himself without fear or reserve into the most intimate relations with students. His conduct was so Christ-like and is so great an example, that it is worthy of being commemorated here.

Professor Tholuck is well known, by name at least, to all who have any tincture of theological knowledge. His numerous works in exegesis and apologetics give him a high place among the evangelical theologians of the century. He ranks still higher as a reforming force. What Wesley did for the Church of England, and

---

them their enthusiasm, enlisting their sympathies, and drawing out their talents. . . . Dr. Chalmers in Glasgow, gathering young men around him, pouring his own views and spirit into them, rousing them to aid in his territorial schemes, and thus training the youths who in after years became the *elite* of the Christian laity of the west, comes as near as may be on a mere common level to the example of Christ and His Twelve."

Chalmers for the Church of Scotland, and Vinet for the Church of Switzerland, he may be said to have done for the Church of Germany: he fought down and annihilated the old Rationalism, which corresponded to our Moderatism, and during the first decades of this century made evangelical religion a respected and waxing power in the land.*

But the method by which he chiefly accomplished this is what will entitle him to lasting remembrance in the Church of God. No sooner was he converted and settled down to his work as an academic teacher, than he at once began to seek intercourse with his students of a kind most unusual in Germany. Not satisfied with merely lecturing from his chair, he made himself personally acquainted with them all, with the view of winning them to Christ. He invited them to walk with him; he visited them in their lodgings; he gathered them in his rooms two evenings a week for prayer, study of the Scriptures and reports of missionary enterprise. As time went on and his classes grew, this became a task of portentous dimensions. But his devotion to it never relaxed. At the busiest period of his life, when he was preparing lectures which filled his classroom with crowds of students and publishing the books which won him a worldwide reputation, he regularly spent four hours a day walking with students, besides having one student at dinner with him and another at supper.

It was not superficial work. It bore no resemblance to the method of some who think they have dealt with a man about his spiritual concerns when they have once forced the subject of religion into conversation without preparation. He often found the approaches to the mind of the student very difficult and had to

---

* The great name of Schleiermacher will doubtless occur to many as deserving to occupy this place; and it would be difficult to overestimate the profundity and extent of his influence. But to me at least the Life of Tholuck (by Witte, 1886) has been a revelation as to what were the real sources of the Evangelical Revival in Germany. Schleiermacher intellectualised the movement and became the scientific guide of those who had been spiritually quickened; but the quickening itself, on which in the last resort all depended, was largely due to humbler instrumentalities.

begin far out on the circumference of things. He was full of geniality and overflowed with humour; he tried the students' wits with the oddest questions, and those who had enjoyed the privilege of walking with him would retail for weeks afterwards the quips and sallies in which he had indulged. He was full of intellectual interest, knew how to draw every man out on the subjects with which he was acquainted, and could give invaluable hints on books and methods of study. He endeavoured to rouse and stimulate the mind from every side, and many owed to him their mental as well as their spiritual awakening. He did not neglect the body either: no professor in Germany did so much to help on poor students. Yet, all the time, he had his eye on one object and was drifting steadily towards it—the personal salvation of every student with whom he had to deal.

He had his reward. It was known in his lifetime that his success had been great; but it is only by the publication of his biography that it has been made known how great it was. Among his papers were found hundreds of letters from students and ministers owning him as their spiritual father; and it turns out that among his converts were some of the most illustrious names in the German literary history of the century. In the pulpits and professorial chairs of Germany there are at present hundreds working for the evangel who owe their souls to him.

Why does such a life seem to us so original and exceptional? Why is it not repeated in other spheres—in the office, the shop and the school, as well as in the Church and the university? Tholuck explained the secret of his life in a single sentence: "I have but one passion, and that is Christ."

XV.

Christ as a Controversialist

Matt.	v. 21-48.
	ix. 10-13.
	xii. 24-45.
	xv. 1-14.
	xvi. 1-4.
	xix. 3-12.
	xxi. 23-46.
	xxii.
	xxiii.
Luke	vii. 36-50.
	x. 25-37.
	xi. 37-54.
	xii. 1.
	xiii. 11-17.
John	ii. 18-20.
	v.
	vi. 41-65.
	vii. 10-53.
	viii. 12-59.

CHAPTER XV.

Christ as a Controversialist.

The ministers of the temple of truth, it has been said, are of three kinds: first, those stationed at the gate of the temple to constrain the passers-by to come in; secondly, those whose function is to accompany inside all who have been persuaded to enter, and display and explain to them the treasures and secrets of the place; and, thirdly, those whose duty is to patrol round the temple, keeping watch and ward and defending the shrine from the attacks of enemies. We are only speaking very roughly if we say that the first of these three functions is that of the Preacher, the second that of the Teacher, and the third that of the Controversialist.

I.

At the present time controversy has an evil name; the mere mention of it excites alarm; and the image of the controversialist, in most people's minds, is anything but an amiable or admired figure. He who is called in providence to undertake the function of controversy can reckon less than almost any other servant of Christ on the sympathy and appreciation of Christ's people; for even those who agree with his view of the truth will be sorry that he has allowed himself to enter the atmosphere of strife, and regret that he has not rested content with other kinds of work. This temper of mind of the Christian public has had its natural result. Able men are shy of undertaking work of this kind, easily finding employment for their talents in other directions, where labour is more appreciated. Controversy has accordingly fallen to a large extent into the hands of inferior practitioners; and it would be easy to mention controversies acknowledged to be of vital consequence to the welfare of the Church which do not receive the support of the champions whose advocacy would lend them dignity in the eyes of men.

It would be interesting to trace this state of public feeling back to its causes; for without doubt there are good reasons for it. It would probably be found to be a reaction from the temper of a time when controversy was carried to excess; for, although an important function of the Church, controversy is far from being the most important; and that which in due proportion is wholesome may in excess be poisonous. In their zeal for truth good men have sometimes forgotten to be zealous for charity. Controversy has raged round small points, on which Christians might well agree to differ, with a heat and violence which would only have been justified had the hearths and altars been at stake. When men thus indulge their passions, they lose from their own minds the sense of proportion, and, having expended their superlatives on objects of trifling importance, they have not the use of them when subjects emerge to which they would be really applicable. They also lose their hold on others; for the public mind, having been flogged into fury over questions which it afterwards discovers were not worth fighting about, refuses to stir even when the citadel is in danger. Thus has the Church to expiate her mistakes.

Yet it is no good sign of the times that controversy should be looked down upon. As has been mentioned in the Preface to this book, we have had to refrain from printing in full the evidence, from the Gospels, of the conduct of Jesus in the different departments of life; but, had this been done, the bulkiest of all these bodies of evidence would have been the appendix to the present chapter. In the records of His life we have pages upon pages of controversy. It may have been far from the work in which He delighted most to be engaged; but He had to undertake it all through His life, and especially towards the close. The most eminent of His servants in every age have had to do the same. St. Paul may not have been indisposed by nature to throw himself into controversy; but St. John had to enter into it with equal earnestness. It is scarcely possible to mention a representative man in any section of the Christian Church in any age who has been able altogether to avoid it.

The spirit of the true controversialist is the joyful and certain sense of possessing the truth, and the conviction of its value to all men, which makes error hateful and inspires the determination to sweep it away.* It was as the King of Truth[†] that Christ carried on controversy, and He was borne along by the generous passion to cut His fellow-men out from their imprisonment in the labyrinth of error. Excessive aversion to controversy may be an indication that a Church has no keen sense of possessing truth which is of any great worth, and that it has lost appreciation for the infinite difference in value between truth and error.

II.

There are differences, indeed, in the present feeling of the public mind to different kinds of controversy. One of the tasks of controversy is to combat error outside of the Church. Christianity is incessantly assailed by forms of unbelief, which arise one after another and have their day. At one time it is Deism which requires

---

* "Late in life he (Mozley) speculated on the controversial temper with an evident though unacknowledged sense of experience. He did not appear to estimate it over-highly, further than as he considered it now to be rare. The contrary temperament was dealt with tenderly—the one that really needs the agreement of those around it, that has a sense of discomfort and privation without it, that must act with others; but the true controversial spirit, that which, strong in the feeling of possession, of a firm hold of its own view, rises with opposition or neglect, which can stand alone, ready as it were for all comers, this was the temper that, as he defined it, his nature evidently responded to."—Introduction to *Mozley's Essays.*

† John xviii. 37.

to be refuted, at another Pantheism, at another Materialism. To defend the temple of Christian truth from such assailants is popular enough and meets with perhaps even excessive rewards. This kind of controversy is accordingly much cultivated and sometimes may be indulged in where it is not needed. When it is of the right quality, however, its value cannot be overestimated; and at the present moment it requires the very highest talent, for the apologetic problems of our century have not yet been solved.

It is controversy within the Church which excites alarm and aversion. Yet the controversy which our Lord waged was inside the Church; and so has been that carried on by the most eminent of His followers. It would, indeed, be well if the sound of controversial weapons were never heard in the temple of peace; but only on condition that it is also a temple of truth. In the time of Christ it was the stronghold of error; and not once or twice since then it has been the same. Jesus had to assail nearly the whole ecclesiastical system of His time and a large body of the Church's doctrines. To do so must, to a thoughtful mind, in any circumstances be an extremely painful task; for the faith reposed in their spiritual guides by the mass of men, who have little leisure or ability to think out vast subjects to the bottom, is one of the most sacred pillars of the edifice of human life; and nothing can be more criminal than wantonly to shake it. But it sometimes needs to be shaken, and Jesus did so.

Of course the opposite case may easily occur: the Church may have the truth, and the innovator may be in error. Then the true place of the Christian controversialist is on the side of the Church against him who is trying to mislead her. This also is a delicate task, requiring the utmost Christian wisdom and sometimes likely to be repaid with little thanks; for, while he who defends the Church against error coming from the outside is loaded with honours as a saviour of the faith, he who attempts to preserve her from more menacing danger within may be dismissed with the odious and withering title of heresy-hunter. But it is not easy to see what ethical standing-ground there is to the competent

Christian man between either, on the one hand, attacking the Church himself as heretical or, on the other, being prepared to defend her from accusations of not teaching the truth.

III.

Christ and the Jewish teachers with whom He contended had a common standard and test of controversies to which they appealed. Both acknowledged the Scriptures of the Old Testament to be the Word of God. As this gave a peculiar colouring to all His work among the Jewish people, whom He addressed as He could not have preached to any other nation, so also it immensely simplified His work as a controversialist. His superiority consisted in His more intimate familiarity with this standard to which they both appealed. They were, indeed, the learned men of the nation, and the Old Testament was their textbook; while He, as they liked to remind Him, had never learned. But His intense love for the Word of His Father and His life-long diligence in searching it made Him far more than a match for them on their own ground. Out of the stores of memory He could fetch the passage which was needed on every occasion; and, as He brought forth the word which was to overthrow their argument, He would sometimes taunt them, who boasted of their acquaintance with the Bible, by beginning His quotation with the question, "Have ye never read?" At other times, in a more solemn mood, He would tell them plainly, "Ye do err, not knowing the Scriptures."

He did not, however, trust merely to His knowledge of the letter of Scripture. This is the method of the small controversialist, who is satisfied if he can always meet text with text and if at the end he has one text more than his opponent. Such controversy is barren as the sand of the sea driven with the wind and has no more value than the bickerings of kites and crows. It is this kind of controversy which has brought the controversial function of the Church into contempt. In the true controversialist there is more than mere familiarity with the text of Scripture: he has a grasp of scriptural principles, a religious experience of his own which interprets the Scripture, and a nearness to God which imparts earnestness and dignity to his work.

The mind of Jesus stood thus above the mere letter of Scripture and handled it with consummate ease and freedom. This was why He scarcely ever quoted a text of the Old Testament without revealing a new meaning in it. It was as if His touch split it asunder and showed the gem flashing at its heart. Sometimes He would gather a principle from the general scope of Scripture which seemed to dissolve and even contradict the mere letter.* While loving and reverencing the Word of His Father with His whole soul, He knew Himself to be the organ of a revelation in which the older one was to be merged, as the light of the stars is lost in the dawn of the morning.

But it was not with Scripture alone that Jesus operated as a controversialist. There is an appeal to the common sense and to the reason of men—an appeal away from the mere pedantry of learning and the citation of authorities—which every controversialist of real mark must be able to make. And, if it can be made in a flash of wit or in an epigram which stamps itself instantly on the memory, the effect is irresistible, when the controversy is carried on before popular judges. Jesus possessed this power in the highest degree, as many of His sayings show. One of the most striking is this, at which "they marvelled, and left Him, and went their way": "Render unto Caesar the things which are Caesar's and unto God the things which are God's."

IV.

In any exposition of the ethics of controversy at the present day, a prominent place would be given to the duty of treating opponents with consideration. However severely their arguments may be handled, their persons ought to be treated with respect, and they should receive credit for honourable motives.

---

* *E.g.*, Matt. v. 31, 33.

No rule could be more reasonable. We know but little of our fellow-men at the best, and, when anything inflames us against them, it is easy to be blinded by prejudice to their excellences. On the other hand, we know so much about ourselves that we may well hesitate to cast stones at others. No man has all the truth, and an opponent may be seeing a side of it which we cannot see. God sometimes gets the whole truth given to the Church only by the halves of it, held by different minds, meeting at first in conflict. The fire generated by their collision unites them at last in perfect fusion.*

Yet, excellent as this rule is, it is not without exceptions; for Jesus broke it. We have not enough information to know whether or not at the beginning of His career He treated His opponents with more consideration; but, towards the end of His life, He exposed them with more and more keenness, and at last He poured on Pharisees, scribes and priests a torrent of scorn never equalled in its withering and annihilating vehemence.†

In point of fact, our estimate of the characters of men exercises an important influence on the value we set on their opinions. We may not be able to express it in public, yet in secret we may know that about an opponent which robs his opinions of all weight. He may be writing or speaking confidently on religious subjects, while we know him to be a thoroughly irreligious man, who has not the very faculty on which true insight in such matters

---

* "They that purify silver to the purpose, use to put it in the fire again and again, that it may be thoroughly tried. So is the truth of God; there is scarce any truth but hath been tried over and over again, and still if any dross happen to mingle with it then God calls it in question again. If in former times there have been Scriptures alleged that have not been pertinent to prove it, that truth shall into the fire again, that what is dross may be burnt up; the Holy Ghost is so curious, so delicate, so exact, He cannot bear that falsehood should be mingled with the truths of the Gospel. That is the reason, therefore, why that God doth still, age after age, call former things in question, because that there is still some dross one way or other mingled with them; either in the stating the opinions themselves, or else in the Scriptures that are brought and alleged for them, that have passed for current, for He will never leave till He have purified them."—Thomas Goodwin.

† Matt. xxiii.

depends, and who could not afford to confess the truth, even if he knew it, because it would condemn himself at every point. It may in certain circumstances be a duty to make this public. Jesus often told the Jewish teachers that it was impossible for them to understand Him, because they lacked moral sympathy with the truth; and the interests of priests and Pharisees were vested in the system of hypocrisy which their arguments were invented to defend. Our judgments in such cases are liable to be mistaken; but He could completely trust His own; and at last He broke all the authority of His opponents by thoroughly exposing their character.

V.

In the very rush of the controversial onset however, Jesus would pause to note and acknowledge a better spirit, if any sign of candour showed itself in an opponent.

There was a day of fierce conflict in His life to which the Evangelists devote close attention. It was one of the days of the last week before He suffered, and a combination of a most formidable character took place among His enemies, to confute Him and put Him down. The scribes and Pharisees were there of course; even the Sadducees, who in general neglected Him, had come out of their haughty retirement; and Pharisees and Herodians, who generally hated one another, were for once united in a common purpose. They had arranged well beforehand the questions with which they were to try Him; they had chosen their champions; and one after another they delivered their assaults upon Him in the Temple. But it was for them a day of disaster and humiliation; for He refuted them so conclusively that "no man was able to answer Him a word; neither durst any man from that day forth ask Him any more questions."

In the very midst, however, of this exciting scene a controversialist arose to whom Jesus extended very different treatment than to the rest. The man appears to have known comparatively little about Christ, except that He was one who was everywhere spoken against. But he was a scribe, and, as his party was attacking Christ, he was drawn into the same attitude. He looked upon Him as a misleader of the people, who deserved to be put down, and he had come to do so. Yet the answers which he heard Jesus giving before his own turn came shook him; for they were right answers, which by no means confirmed the impressions of Christ which he had brought to the spot. Some such acknowledgment seems to have been conveyed in the tone of his own question, when he put it.

It was, indeed, but a paltry question, "Which is the first commandment of all?" This was one of the subjects on which in the rabbinical schools they were wont to chop logic, and the man probably considered that it was one on which he was superior to any other rabbi. Jesus, however, had observed something that pleased Him in the man's look or manner, and, instead of merely overthrowing and humiliating him, as He had done to the others, He gave him a full and earnest answer: "The first of all the commandments is, Hear, O Israel; The Lord our God is one Lord: and thou shalt love the Lord thy God with all thy heart, and with all thy soul, and with all thy mind: this is the first commandment. And the second is like, namely this, Thou shalt love thy neighbour as thyself. There is none other commandment greater than these."

To us this is familiar teaching, and it falls on our senses without making much impression. But it is not difficult to conceive with what irresistible power and majesty it may have fallen on a mind which heard it for the first time. It seems to have thrown the man completely out of the cavilling attitude into one of intense moral earnestness. It not only smote his arguments down, but burst open the doors of his being and went straight to his conscience, which sent back the echo instantaneously and clearly: "Well, Master, Thou hast said the truth: for there is one God; and there is none other but He: and to love Him with all the heart, and with all the understanding, and with all the soul, and with all the strength, and to love his neighbour as himself, is more than all whole burnt offerings and sacrifices."

This was a noble answer. The man had forgotten the role he had come to play; he had forgotten his comrades, and what they were expecting of him; he let his heart speak and did homage to the moral dignity of Christ. Jesus marked the change with deep inward satisfaction and said to him, "Thou art not far from the kingdom of God."

This is a great example. To attack them remorselessly in controversy often drives into permanent opposition those who might be won by milder treatment. Men may appear as opponents of Christianity who in their hearts are very near it; and it is Christlike to detect this sympathy and bring it to expression. To prove to men that they are outside the kingdom is an easy thing in comparison; but it may be far better to let them see that they are only a few steps from its threshold. The triumph of a ruthless polemic may gratify the natural heart; but far more like the Master, where it is possible, is a winning irenicum.

XVI.

Christ as a Man of Feeling

Matt.	viii. 17.	Matt.	xxvii. 34.
	ix. 36.	Mark	x. 13-16; 21.
	xiv. 14.		xii. 34.
	xv. 32.	Luke	x. 21.
	xx. 34.		xix. 41.
Mark	i. 41.	John	viii. 1-11.
	iv. 33.		xii. 27.
Luke	vii. 11-15.		xiii. 21.
			xx. 16, 17.
Matt.	viii. 10.		
	ix. 2, 28.	Matt.	viii. 4.
	xi. 6.		ix. 30.
	xiii. 58.		xii. 16.
	xiv. 31.		xiv. 22.
	xv. 28.		xvi. 20.
	xxvi. 13, 38.		xvii. 9.
Mark	vi. 5, 6.	Mark	vii. 24, 36.
	viii. 12.		viii. 26, 30.
Luke	vii. 9.	John	v. 13.
	xvii. 17.		vi. 15.

Matt.	xvi. 23.
	xvii. 17.
	xxvi. 50, 55.
Mark	i. 25.
	iii. 5.
	xv. 3, 5.
Luke	iv. 35; 39-41.
John	xi. 33-38.

CHAPTER XVI.

Christ as a Man of Feeling.

So much learning has been expended in the present age on the Life of Christ, and every particle of the record has been so thoroughly sifted, that it may be questioned if mere intellect will now discover much that is new in the subject. There may still, however, be great scope for the divinatory power of feeling.* Jesus was as refined and delicate in feeling as He was wise in speech and mighty in act; and the motives of His conduct are often incomprehensible except to those who possess in some degree the same feelings as He had. He taught mankind to feel finely, and ever since He was in the world there have been increasing numbers who have learned from Him to regard child-hood and woman, poverty and service, and many other objects,

---

* No more brilliant instance of such psychological interpretation could be adduced than the explanation given in *Ecce Homo* of our Lord's conduct when the woman taken in adultery was brought to Him. "He stooped down and wrote on the ground" (John viii. 8). Why did He do so? It was because He was ashamed of listening to a foul story. "He was seized with an intolerable sense of shame. He could not meet the eye of the crowd, or of the accusers, and perhaps at that moment least of all of the woman. . . . In His burning embarrassment and confusion He stooped down so as to hide His face, and began writing with His finger on the ground." Everyone who reads this explanation feels it to be the true one; it shines with its own light; and, when first heard, gives a shock of delighted surprise.

The author adds, "The effect on Jesus was such as might have been produced upon many men since, but perhaps scarcely upon any man that ever lived before."

with sentiments totally different from those with which they were regarded before His advent.

The notices in the Gospels of the impressions made on His feelings by different situations in which He was placed are extraordinarily numerous; but a single incident—the raising of the daughter of Jairus—in which the feelings of His heart came conspicuously into view will serve as a sufficient clue.

I.

His Compassion was illustrated in this incident.

It was the case of a man whose only daughter was lying at the point of death; and he besought Jesus greatly for her, says St. Mark. The heart of Jesus could not but answer such an appeal. In a similar instance—that of a woman with an only son, the widow of Nain—it is said that, when the Lord saw her following behind the bier, He had compassion on her and said to her, "Weep not." He not only gave the required help in such cases, but gave it with an amount of sympathy which doubled its value. Thus He not only raised Lazarus, but wept with his sisters. In curing a man who was deaf, He sighed as He said, "Ephphatha." All His healing work cost Him feeling. There is a great difference between the clergyman or physician who merely calls at the house of sorrow as a matter of duty, to be able to say that he has been there, and him who takes the suffering of the stricken home on his heart and goes away melted and broken down with it.

On this occasion the compassion of Christ was deepened by the fact that it was a child who was ill. "My little daughter" she was called by her father. All the scenes in Christ's life in which children appear are exquisitely touching; and it was His feeling which gave them their beauty and pathos. As you look at them, you feel that He not only knew all that is in a father's and a mother's heart, but sank new wells in the heart of humanity and brought love up from deeper levels than it had sprung from before. Ruskin has observed that there are no children in Greek art, but that they abound in Christian art—an unmistakable token that it was the eye of Christ which first fully appreciated the attractiveness of childhood.

II.

A second feeling which Jesus showed in this incident was Sensitiveness.

At Jairus' .request He went to the house where the dying girl was; but on the way a messenger met them, who told the poor father that all was over, and that he need not trouble the Master any further. Whereupon, without waiting to be appealed to, Jesus turned to him and said, "Be not afraid; only believe."

In this we might see a new instance of His compassion; but it also reveals something else: Jesus was extremely sensitive to the sentiments of trust or distrust with which He was regarded. If any generosity of belief was shown towards Him, His heart filled with gladness, and He acknowledged His gratification without stint. Thus, when another applicant for help, in a situation not unlike that of Jairus, expressed his belief that, if Jesus would only speak a word even at a distance, without going to the house in which the sick person was lying, a cure would ensue, Jesus stood still in the road and, turning to the bystanders, exclaimed, "I have not found so great faith, no, not in Israel." The faith of Jairus, though not so strong as this, had evidently gratified Him, and it was because He could not bear to have it clouded with doubt that He hastened so promptly to strengthen it.

He had, however, many an experience to encounter of the opposite kind, and the feeling thereby occasioned in Him was keen. If now and then He had to marvel at the greatness of faith, He had to marvel far oftener at unbelief. In His own native place, when He visited it, He could do scarcely any mighty works on this account. The rebuff so chilled His heart that the activity of His miraculous power was restrained. His most signal favours were sometimes received with ingratitude, as in the case of the ten lepers, of whom only one returned to give thanks for his cure, causing Him to ask sadly, "Where are the nine?"

III.

A third species of feeling which He betrayed on this occasion was Indignation.

When He reached the house, not only was the child dead, but the place had been taken possession of by the mummers who undertook the ghastly ceremonial of mourning. Death, though the most solemn of all events, has in many countries been invested with absurdity through the mourning customs with which it has been associated; but in Palestine this was carried to an extreme. As soon as a death took place, the house was invaded by professional mourners, who filled it with wild ululations and doleful music. This hideous custom was in full operation when Jesus arrived, and to His serene soul it was intolerable. He indignantly enjoined silence, and, when this was not forthcoming, He drove the whole ghastly apparatus forth and cleared the house.

Indignation, though closely allied to sinful anger, is not vicious, but virtuous. It is the sign of an honourable and self-respecting nature. The soul that loves order, uprightness and nobleness cannot but be indignant at disorder, duplicity and meanness. The indignation of Jesus is often mentioned. It could be aroused by unseemly noise and confusion, as on this occasion. When casting out devils, he used angrily to rebuke the outcries of the possessed. He is represented in the same attitude when calming the winds and waves in the storm, presumably because He was counteracting the prince of the power of the air. The whole empire of Satan is the empire of disorder, and every manifestation of its power affected Him in this way. This explains the strange tumult of indignant excitement in which He advanced to the grave of Lazarus: His condition of mind was one of angry vengeance against the ravages of death.*

---

* The story of the raising of Lazarus so abounds with notices of Christ's emotions that we might have taken it for our clue instead of the raising of the daughter of Jairus. As He approached the grave of Lazarus, it is said "He groaned in spirit, and was troubled;" but the Greek words are much stronger: ἐνεβριμήσατο τῷ πνεύματι καὶ ἐτάραξεν ἑαυτόν. The first verb denotes, not groaning, but "vis-

The state of the times in which He lived afforded peculiar occasion for the display of this sentiment. It was because the mourning in the house of Jairus was professional, with no heart in it, that He disliked it so utterly. But the society of Judæa at that time was one vast hypocrisy. The holders of sacred offices were self-seekers; the professors of piety were hunting for the praise of men; the teachers of the people laid grievous burdens on other men's shoulders, which they would not themselves touch with one of their fingers; sacred language was a cloak for spoliation and impurity. Jesus burned with indignation against it all and poured His feelings out in philippics against the parties and per-sonalities of the time.

His was holy fire: it was the flame of truth consuming false-hood, of justice attacking wrong, of love burning against selfish-ness. Too often the crusade against shams and hypocrisy has been inspired by zeal which is unholy. Men have undertaken the office of the censor and satirist whose own hearts have not been pure and whose lives have been inconsistent, plucking the mote out of their brother's eye, and behold a beam was in their own. They have only masqueraded in the garment of indignation. But this robe found in Jesus its true wearer, and He wore it with incomparable

---

ibly-expressed indignation, displeasure, or wrath;" and the second denotes the change in His countenance caused by this indignation. "His whole frame was moved. A storm of wrath was seen to sweep over Him." What was the cause of this angry agitation? "He was gazing into the skeleton face of the world, and trac-ing everywhere the reign of death. The whole earth to Him was but 'the valley of the shadow of death;' and in those tears which were shed in His presence He saw that

> 'Ocean of Time, whose waters of deep woe
> Are brackish with the salt of human tears.'

. . . But this is not all. Behind the presence of death there was the awful real-ity, not only of sin, 'the sting of death,' but also of him through whom sin came,—him who is in this Gospel so frequently called 'the prince of this world.' If then we would rightly understand the true meaning of our Lord's wrath, His visibly-expressed indignation, we must regard Him here as confronting in con-flict the great enemy of His kingdom,—the destroyer of the race which He Himself had come to save."

See a remarkable paper on this difficult passage by the Rev. John Hutchison, D.D., in the *Monthly Interpreter*, vol. ii (T. & T. Clark, 1885).

dignity. "Are ye come out," He demanded of those about to arrest Him, "as against a thief?" "Judas," He asked the traitor, "betrayest thou the Son of man with a kiss?" Before the high-priest, Pilate and Herod His indignant silence was more eloquent than the most scorching words. He has not put off this garment yet: in heaven still burns "the wrath of the Lamb."

IV.

A fourth mode of feeling characteristic of Jesus which was illustrated on this occasion was Delicacy.

Having put the professional mourners out, He went into the room of death, where the little maid was lying on the bed. But He did not go alone, or only with the three disciples whom He had taken into the house with Him: He took with Him the father and mother of the maiden, as being deeply interested in her who was their own and entitled to see all that happened to her.

Then He took her by the hand before pronouncing the resurrection words; for He did not wish her to be startled when she woke, but to feel the support of a sympathetic presence. Many a one in an hour of agitation or when coming out of a swoon has felt how it steadies and strengthens to be held by a firm hand and to look into a calm face.

Thus He did all with perfect tact, not by calculation, but with the instinct of delicate feeling, which guided Him at every turn to do precisely the best thing. Yet there was no straining after refinement. The besetting sin of emotional natures is to overstrain and overdo. But how healthy and manly was the feeling of Jesus! His very next act, after these exquisite touches, was this: "He commanded that something should be given her to eat." In the same way, after days of healing and preaching in the wilderness, during which He had been borne along with the prophetic enthusiasm, it was He who made the proposal that food should be given to the multitude, before they were dispersed, lest they should faint by the way; the disciples, though far less preoccupied, never thinking of such a thing. He excelled them as much in considerateness and practicality as in delicacy of feeling.

V.

The last kind of feeling exhibited by our Lord on this occasion was Modesty.

After the miracle was performed, "He charged them straitly that no man should know it." This is the sequel to many a work of wonder in His life. "See thou tell no man," He said to a leper whom He had cleansed. "See that no man know it," He said to two blind men whose sight He had restored. He straitly charged those, as a rule, out of whom He had cast devils not to make Him known.

Such notices abound in the Gospels; yet I am not sure that I have ever seen the true explanation of them given. All kinds of elaborate explanations have been attempted. In one case, for example, it is said that He forbade the man who had been healed to mention his cure, lest it should do him harm by puffing him up; in another, because his testimony would have had no weight; in a third, because it was not yet time to acknowledge Himself to be the Messiah; and so on. Such are the suggestions made by learned men, and there may be some truth in them all. But they are too elaborate and recondite; the real explanation lies on the surface. It is simply that, while so great a worker, He disliked to have His good deeds made known. St. Matthew puts this so plainly that it ought not to have been overlooked. After mentioning an occasion when, after healing great multitudes, He charged them that they should not make Him known, the evangelist adds that this was in fulfilment of a prophecy which said, "He shall not strive nor cry, neither shall any one hear His voice in the street." It is one of the penalties of public work for God that it comes to be talked about, and vulgar people make a sensation of it. We are well acquainted with this at the present day, when nothing is allowed to remain private, and, if a man does anything in the least out of the common, the minutest details of his life are dragged out and exposed to the public eye. But this is contrary to the very genius of goodness and exposes even those occupied with the holiest work to the temptation of playing for the praise of men instead of acting humbly in the eye of God. Jesus detested it. He would have been hidden if He could; and it was a heavy cross to Him that the more He pressed people to say nothing about Him, the more widely did they spread His fame.*

Such was the heart of Christ as it is laid bare in a single story. By taking a wider sweep we might have accumulated more illustrations. But the clue, once seized, can be easily followed in the Gospels, where the notices of how He felt in the different situations in which He was placed are far more numerous than anyone whose attention has not been specially directed to them would believe.†

Nor would it be difficult to trace the refining influence which intercourse with Him had on His disciples—how they learned to feel about things as He did. There is no other influence so refining as genuine religion. Where the Gospel is faithfully preached and affectionately believed, there is gradually wrought into the very features of people the stamp of the Son of man. The friendship of Jesus breeds the gentle heart.

---

* There is, however, a shrinking from publicity which is vicious: it may be mere fastidiousness or the cowardice which fears responsibility. And there is an enjoyment of popularity which is nothing but unselfish absorption in the triumph of a good cause.

† "Christus multum et vultu et nutu docuit"—BENGEL.

XVII.

Christ as an Influence

Matt.	vii. 28.	Mark	i. 23-27.
	viii. 27.		v. 6, 7.
	ix. 8, 26, 31,	Luke	vi. 11.
	33.		xiii. 14.
	xii. 23.		
	xiii. 54.	Matt.	ii. 1-3.
	xxii. 22, 33.		iii. 13, 14.
Mark	i. 45.		iv. 19-22.
	ii. 1, 2, 12.		xxvii. 19, 55.
	vii. 36, 37.	Mark	i. 37.
	ix. 15.		v. 18.
	xv. 5.		xii. 37.
Luke	ii. 47, 48.	Luke	i. 41.
	iv. 15, 22, 32,		viii. 40.
	37.		xi. 27.
			xxii. 61, 62.
Matt.	xiv. 1, 2.		xxiv. 32.
Mark	iv. 41.	John	vi. 68.
	x. 32.		vii.
Luke	v. 8, 26.		
	xxiii. 45, 48.		
John	xviii. 6.		

CHAPTER XVII.

Christ as an Influence.

In the foregoing chapter we have seen the feelings produced in the sensitive heart of Christ by the persons and things He was brought into contact with. In the present one we have to deal with the feelings which He produced, by His presence and actions, in the hearts of men. If much attention is paid in the records of His life to the depth and variety of the impressions which others made on Him, no less surprising is the number of notices they contain of the impressions which He made on others.

Simeon the aged, when he held the child Jesus in his arms in the Temple, prophesied that by contact with Him the thoughts of many hearts would be revealed; and this was one of the most out-standing features of His subsequent life. None who came near Him could remain indifferent. They might hate or they might love, they might admire or they might scorn Him; but in any case they were compelled to show the deepest that was in them. In the Talmud there is a fable that King Solomon wore a ring engraven with the divine name, and everyone towards whom he turned the inscription was forced to speak out whatever he was thinking at the moment. So Jesus, by His mere presence among men, brought to the surface their deepest thoughts and feelings and made them display the best and the worst which their hearts concealed.

I.

The commonest impression which He is narrated in the Gospels to have excited is Wonder. "They marvelled at Him;" "they wondered;" "they were astonished with a great astonishment"—such are the phrases which recur continually in the records of His life. Sometimes it was at His teaching that they marvelled—at its gracefulness, originality and power—or at the knowledge displayed by one who had never learned. Still more noisy was their wonder at His miracles. People ran together to the spot where a miracle was taking place; those who had been cured spread abroad the fame of what had happened to themselves; and, wherever He went, there rose around Him a cloud of notoriety.

Though this was the commonest impression made on people's minds, it was far from the most valuable. To Himself it was an unpleasant necessity. His soul shrank from the importunities of the crowd, and He gauged the depth of their shallow adulation. The one advantage of it, for the sake of which He submitted to the necessity, was that it brought to Him, among the rest, those who really wanted Him and whom He wanted—as in the case of the woman who came behind Him in the crowd, when He was on the way to the house of Jairus, and touched the hem of His garment, that she might be healed. The crowd was thronging Him, many no doubt touching His very person; but they got nothing from this contact. She came in dire need and trembling faith, and, at her touch, virtue went out of Him and healed her. But she would hardly have been there but for the crowd: it was by the noise and excitement that she was informed that He was near; at all events the crowd supplied her with her opportunity.

This may still be the one advantage which compensates for the many drawbacks of the rumour that rises round religion in some of its forms. The sensation is a bell that rings into church those who need Christ. The appearance of popular preachers is trumpeted abroad, and crowds flock to hear them. When a distinguished evangelist appears or a revival of religion breaks out, the country is moved with wonder. Much of this noise is silly enough, but some may derive advantage from it. While the multitudes throng, one here and there touches. The crowd comes talking and buzzing out of church, but someone, hurrying silently through the throng to escape into solitude, carries away a blessing.

II.

Sometimes wonder deepened into Fear. Thus, when He rose from sleep during the storm and rebuked the winds and waves, it is said, "they feared exceedingly;" and, when He raised to life the widow's son at Nain, "there came a fear on all."

From other parts of Scripture also it may be inferred that this was the natural result of witnessing a miracle. A miracle, seen close at hand, produced the sense of the immediate presence of the Almighty; and any unmistakable manifestation of the divine excites fear. At loud and sudden thunder there falls an awe over the spirit; and I have heard those who have experienced an earthquake describe the sensation of terror it awakens as unique and quite beyond the control of the will. It is the sense of being utterly helpless in the grasp of immeasurable power. Those who saw Christ perform a miracle felt that there was in Him that which could do what it pleased with them and with nature round about them; and it was this vague impression of the divine in Him which made them afraid.

But the fear He inspired was at other times a genuine tribute to the majesty of His human character; and we get no more authentic glimpses of the moral stature of Jesus than by observing the impressions which He produced on the minds of others in the great moments of His life. At the gate of Gethsemane, when He encountered the band sent to arrest Him, the traces of the experiences which He had passed through in the garden were still upon Him, and the effect of His rapt and tragic air was extraordinary. At the sight of Him "they went backward and fell to the ground." All through the last six months of His life, indeed, He seems habitually to have been invested, through brooding on His approaching fate, with an awful dignity. His great purpose sharpened His features, straightened His figure and quickened His step; and sometimes, as He pushed ahead of the Twelve, absorbed in His own thoughts, "they were amazed; and, as they followed, they were afraid."

Earlier, however, even in the serene beginning of His ministry, there were manifestations of this overpowering moral dignity. When He drove the buyers and sellers out of the Temple, in the first access of His prophetic inspiration, why did they flee crouching before Him? They were many, while He was but one; they were wealthy and influential, while He was but a peasant. Yet there was that in Him which they never thought of resisting. They felt how awful goodness is. There is a majesty in virtue indignant before which the loftiest sinners cower. I have known a youth from the country enter an office in the city, where the daily conversation was so foul and profane that it would almost have disgraced the hulks; but a month after his arrival not a man in the place dared to utter an unchaste word when he was present. Yet he had scarcely spoken a syllable of reproof; it was simply the dignity of manly goodness that quelled conscious iniquity.

III.

The fear excited by Jesus sometimes deepened into Repulsion. The fear He caused was the fear of the finite in the grasp of the Infinite. But those who felt themselves helpless in the hands of the Almighty felt themselves at the same time exposed in the sight of the All-seeing and the All-pure.

As the ignorant speak with fluency in the company of the ignorant, but, if introduced among the learned, stammer and become afraid of their own voices; or as the beggar, who is quite unconscious of his rags when moving among his equals, if brought into a drawing-room filled with well-dressed people, becomes suddenly aware of every patch on his coat and every hole in his looped and windowed raggedness; so, when confronted with spotless holiness, the human soul turns round upon itself and recognises its imperfections. It was this which made St. Peter, when he saw the miraculous draught of fishes, put up his hands in deprecation and cry to Jesus, "Depart from me, for I am a sinful man, O Lord." And for the same reason the Gadarenes, when they beheld the miracle which Jesus had wrought in their midst, besought Him to depart out of their coasts. They felt the instinctive shrinking of the guilty from the holy.

In the tragedy of *Faust*, Margaret, who is meant to represent virgin purity, cannot bear the sight of Mephistopheles, though he is disguised as a knight and she has no idea who he really is. She shrinks from him instinctively:—

> In all my life not anything
> Has given my heart so sharp a sting
> As that man's loathsome visage.

Christ's presence produced precisely the opposite effect: in the unholy it awoke repulsion and the desire to flee from Him. As He held down His head with burning shame and wrote on the ground, when the sinful woman was brought to Him, her accusers, at length dimly recognising what was going on in His mind, grew afraid and, "being convicted in their own conscience, went out one by one, beginning at the eldest, even unto the last; and Jesus was left alone, and the woman standing in the midst." When He drew near to possessed persons, His mere proximity threw them into paroxysms of excitement, and they entreated Him to depart and not torment them; for merely to see one so holy was a torment.

The presence of superlative goodness, if it does not subdue, stirs up the wild beasts which lurk in the subterranean caverns of the human heart into angry opposition to itself. Christ made the evil in those who opposed Him show itself at its very worst. Pilate, for example, only applied to the case of Jesus the same principles of administration which he had made use of in hundreds of other cases—the principles of the self-seeker and time-server dressed in the garb of justice; but never did these principles appear in all their ghastly unrighteousness till he released Barabbas and handed over Jesus to the executioner. The inhumanity and hollowness of Sadducee and Pharisee were never seen in their true colours till the light which streamed from Jesus fell on them and exposed every spot and wrinkle of the hypocrite's robe. Christ's very meekness provoked them to deeper scorn of His pretensions; His silence under their accusations made them gnash their teeth with baffled malice; the castigation of His polemic made them cling to their errors with more desperate tenacity.

Thus are hearts hardened by the very excellence of those with whom they have to deal. As Ahab, when he met Elijah, hissed at him, "Hast thou found me, O mine enemy?" so the mere sense that his godly mother is praying for him, or that good people are planning for his spiritual welfare, may excite in one who is going determinedly down the broad road a diabolical scorn and rage. The contempt with which one who bears witness for God is flouted by his comrades is often only an evidence that they feel his presence a reproach to their own evil characters, and it is a real, though undesigned, tribute to his superiority. "Marvel not if the world hate you; ye know that it hated Me before it hated you."

IV.

Although the presence of Jesus repelled some, it exerted on others the most powerful attraction, and the most characteristic feature of His character was Moral Attractiveness. He repelled those who were wedded to their sins and unwilling to abandon them, but He attracted all who in any degree were feeling after a new and better life.

Strong as the power of sin is in the soul of man, it never altogether overcomes the opposite principle. There is that in every man which opposes his sin and protests against it. It reminds the prodigal of the Father's house, from which he has wandered, and makes him feel the shame of serving among the swine. It warns him in solitary hours that the sin to which he is attached is his worst enemy, and that he will never be happy till he is separated from it.

This redeeming principle in human nature is the conscience; and without its feeling for what is holy and divine the condition of man would be hopeless. But it exists even in the wicked; who cannot withhold their admiration from the truly good and, though following the worse, approve the better, course. It makes men afraid and ashamed of their own sin, even when they are most abandoned to it. It may be stimulated by denunciations of sin, like those of the Baptist; but it is touched even more effectively by the sight of exceptional purity or by the compassion which pities ungodliness. This reminds man of something he has lost; it causes the sinful enjoyments with which he is occupied to appear cheap and vulgar; it makes him uneasy and dissatisfied.

Jesus naturally exerted this kind of influence in the strongest degree. Wherever there existed any tenderness or susceptibility towards what is high and pure, it was stimulated by His presence. Conscience, hearing His voice in its prison, woke up and came to the windows to demand emancipation. As the presence of a physician armed with a cure for some virulent disease excites a sensation among those afflicted with the malady, who communicate the news of relief to one another with the swiftness of a secret telegraphy, so, wherever Jesus went, the heavy-laden and the aspiring heard of Him and found Him. In publicans and sinners, and even in Pharisees, unaccustomed movements showed themselves: Nicodemus sought Him by night; Zacchæus climbed into the sycamore tree to see Him; the woman who was a sinner stole to His feet to bathe them with her tears.

Moral attractiveness is of two kinds—the passive and the active.

There is a goodness which draws men by the mere force of its own beauty. It is not thinking of any such effect; for it is inward and self-absorbed; its attention is concentrated on an inner vision and occupied with following a secret law. It would never think of crediting itself with an influence on others; for it is not aware of its own beauty, and that which sets off all its qualities is the ornament of humility. This is the goodness especially of the feminine virtues, and the characters which exhibit it in a marked degree have always a womanly element. "Such have many of us seen— sometimes in humble life, faithful and devoted, loyal to man and full of melody in their hearts to God, their life one act of praise; some in a higher sphere, living amid the pride of life, but wholly untouched by its spells; free and unensnared souls, that had never been lighted up with the false lights and aspirations of human life, or been fascinated by the evil of the world, though sympathizing with all that is good in it, and enjoying it becomingly; who give us, as far as human character now can do, an insight into the realms of light, the light that comes from neither sun nor moon, but from Him who is the light everlasting."*

Of such characters Jesus is the head and crown. His image shines through all the centuries with the beauty of holiness. This is why the eyes of men, sweeping the fields of history in search of excellence, always rest at last on Him as its perfect and final embodiment. This is why none can write of Christ without falling into a kind of rapture and ecstasy of admiration, and even those who are bitter and blustering in their opposition to everything Christian grow hushed and reverent when they speak of Christ Himself. No pen can fully render the impression made on the reader by His life in the Gospels. It is easy to make a catalogue of the qualities which entered into His human character; but the blending and the harmony and the perfection, the delight and the subduing charm, who can express? Yet all this walked the earth in the flesh, and men and women saw it with their eyes!

The moral attractiveness of the active sort influences in a different way. There are natures which we call magnetic. People cannot help being drawn to them and following where they go. Whatever such natures do, they act with all their might, and others are drawn into the rush and current of their course. It may be

---

* Mozley, *University Sermons.*

an evil course, and then they are ring-leaders in sin; for the kingdom of darkness has its missionaries as well as the kingdom of heaven. Like other forces of human nature, this one requires to be redeemed and consecrated. Then it becomes the spirit of the missionary, the apostle, the religious pioneer.

Nothing in the memoirs of Jesus is more surprising than the apparent ease with which He induced men to quit their occupations and follow Him. John and James are in their ship mending their nets; but, when He calls, they instantly leave the ship and nets and their father Zebedee and go after Him. Matthew is at the seat of custom, and that is a seat not easily left; but no sooner is he called than he forsakes all and follows Jesus. Zacchæus, who had been an extortioner for a lifetime, was no sooner asked to receive Him into his house than he began to make proposals and promises of the utmost generosity. Jesus was engaged in a splendid work, whose idea and results touched the imagination of all who were capable of anything noble. He was wholly absorbed in it; and to see unselfish devotion always awakens imitation. He was the author and leader of a new movement, which grew around Him, and the enthusiasm of those who had joined it drew others in. The same power has belonged in remarkable measure to all great spiritual leaders—to St. Paul, to Savonarola, to Luther, to Wesley and many more; who, filled themselves with the Holy Ghost, have been able to lift men above the instincts of pleasure and comfort and make them willing to deny themselves for a great cause. And no earnest life, in which the enthusiasm of Jesus burns, fails to exercise in some degree the same influence.

It is one of the healthiest features of our day that all thinking people are growing sensitive about their influence. To many the chief dread of sin arises from perceiving that they cannot sin themselves without directly or indirectly involving others; and it would be to them the greatest of satisfactions to be able to believe that they are doing good to those with whom they are brought into contact, and not harm.

This is a feeling worthy of the solemn nature of our earthly existence, and it ought certainly to be one of the guiding principles of life. Yet it is not without its dangers. If allowed too prominent a place among our motives, it would crush the mind with an intolerable weight and cause conduct to appear so responsible that the spring of energy would be broken. It might easily betray us into living so much for effect as to fall into hypocrisy. The healthiest influence is unsought and unconscious. It is not always when we are trying to impress others that we impress them most. They elude the direct efforts which we make, but they are observing us when we are not thinking of it. They detect from an unconscious gesture or chance word the secret we are trying to conceal. They know quite well whether our being is a palace fair within or only a shabby structure with a pretentious elevation. They estimate the mass and weight of our character with curious accuracy; and it is this alone that really tells. Our influence is the precise equivalent of our human worth or worthlessness.

A man may strive for influence and miss it. But let him grow within himself—in self-control, in conscientiousness, in purity and submission—and then he will not miss it. Every step of inward progress makes us worth more to the world and to every cause with which we may be identified. The road to influence is simply the highway of duty and loyalty. Let a man press nearer to Christ and open his nature more widely to admit the energy of Christ, and, whether he knows it or not—it is better perhaps if he does not know it—he will certainly be growing in power for God with men, and for men with God. "Abide in Me, and I in you: as the branch cannot bear fruit of itself except it abide in the vine, no more can ye except ye abide in Me."

Finis.